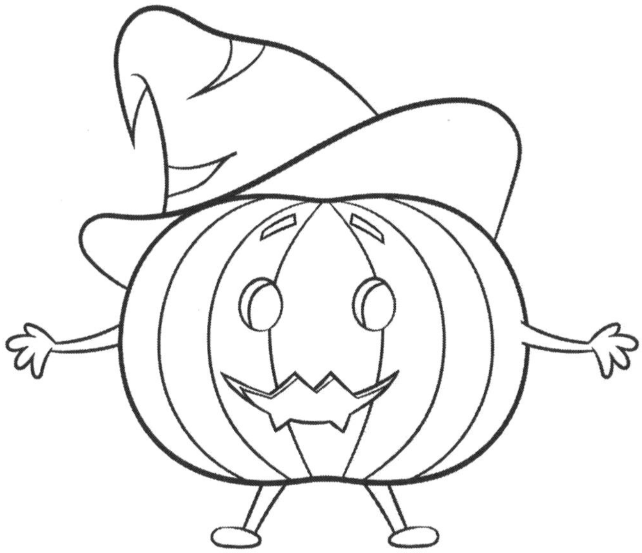

Happy Halloween

Coloring Book for Toddlers

Blue Wave Press

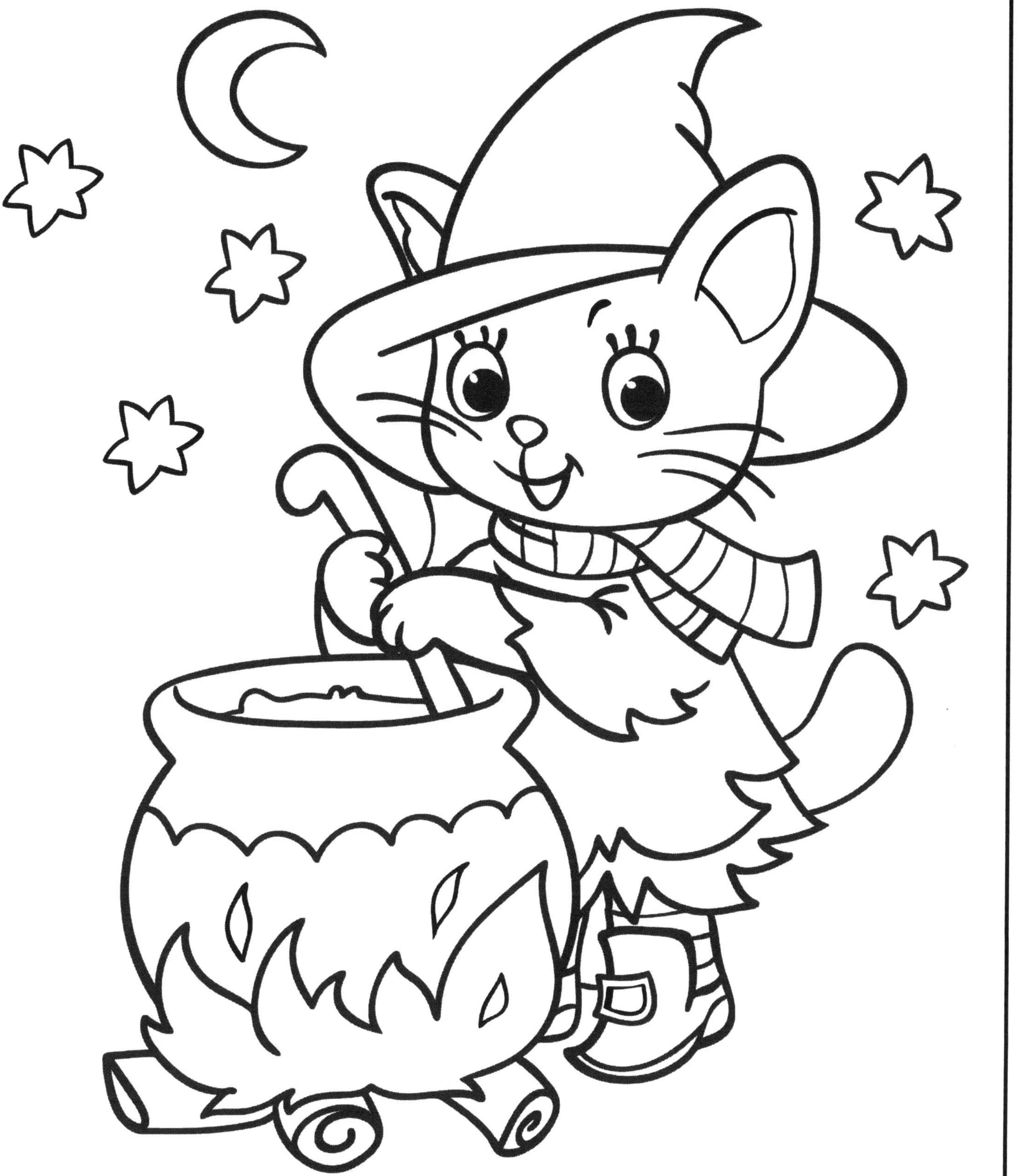

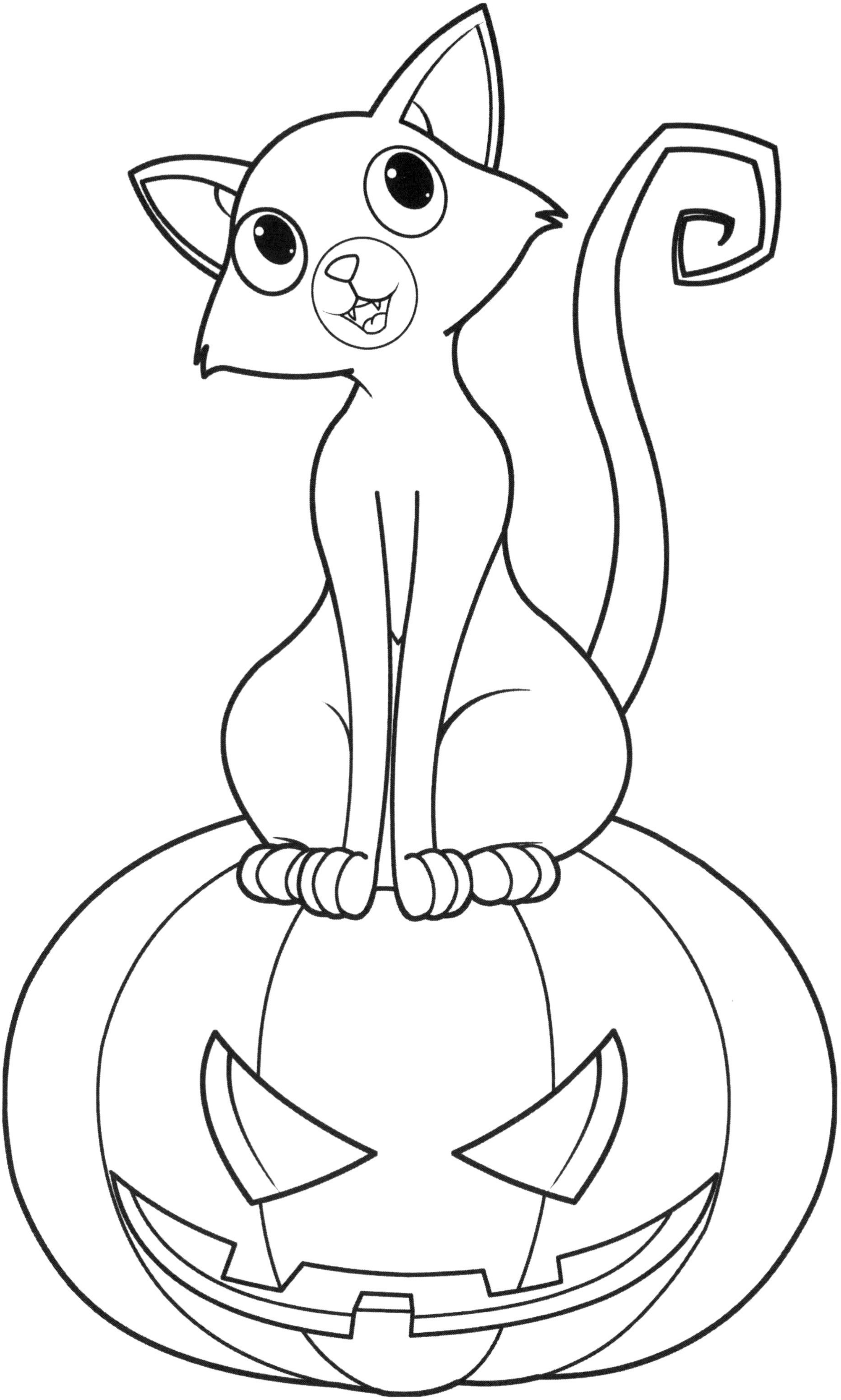

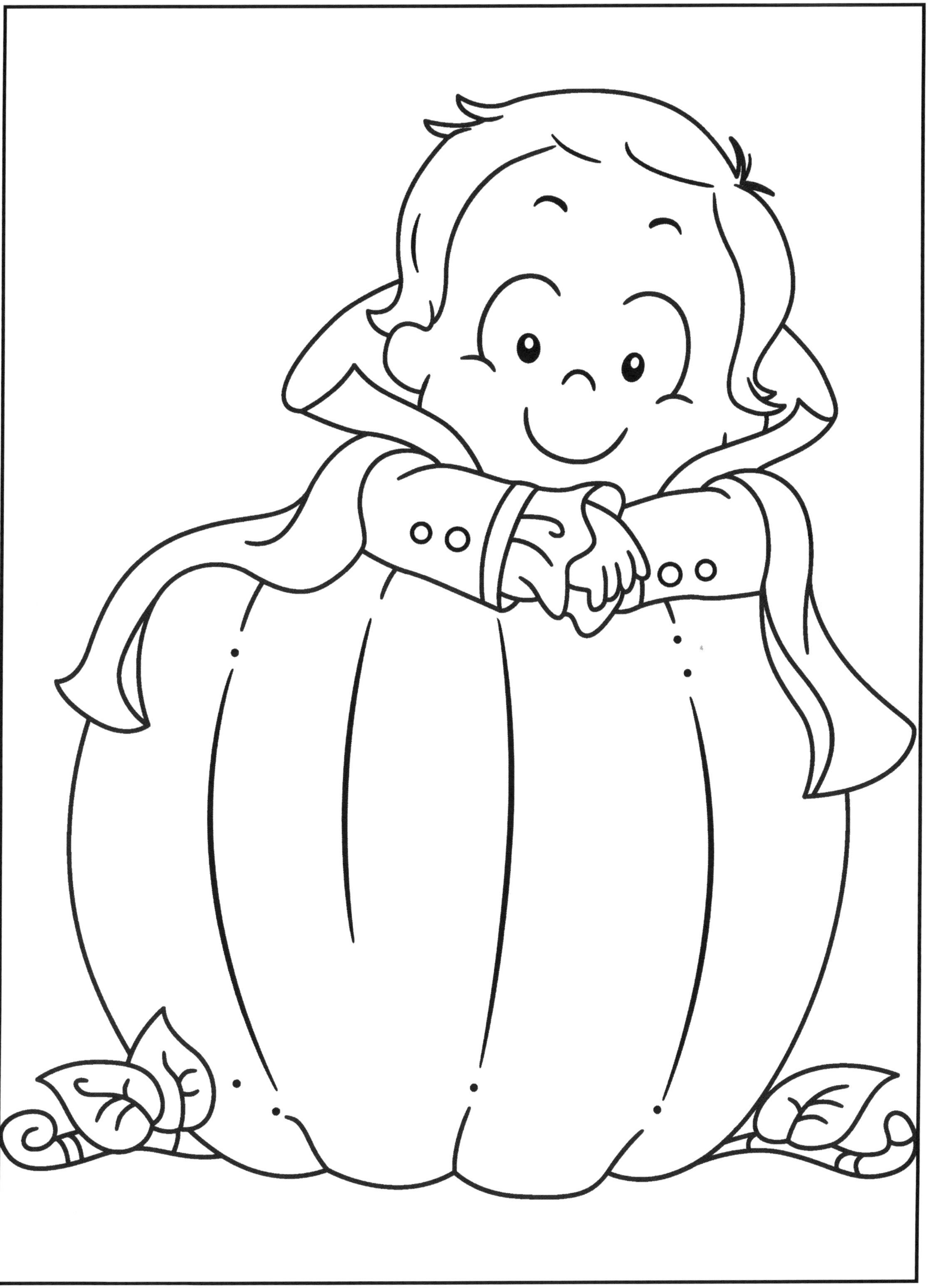

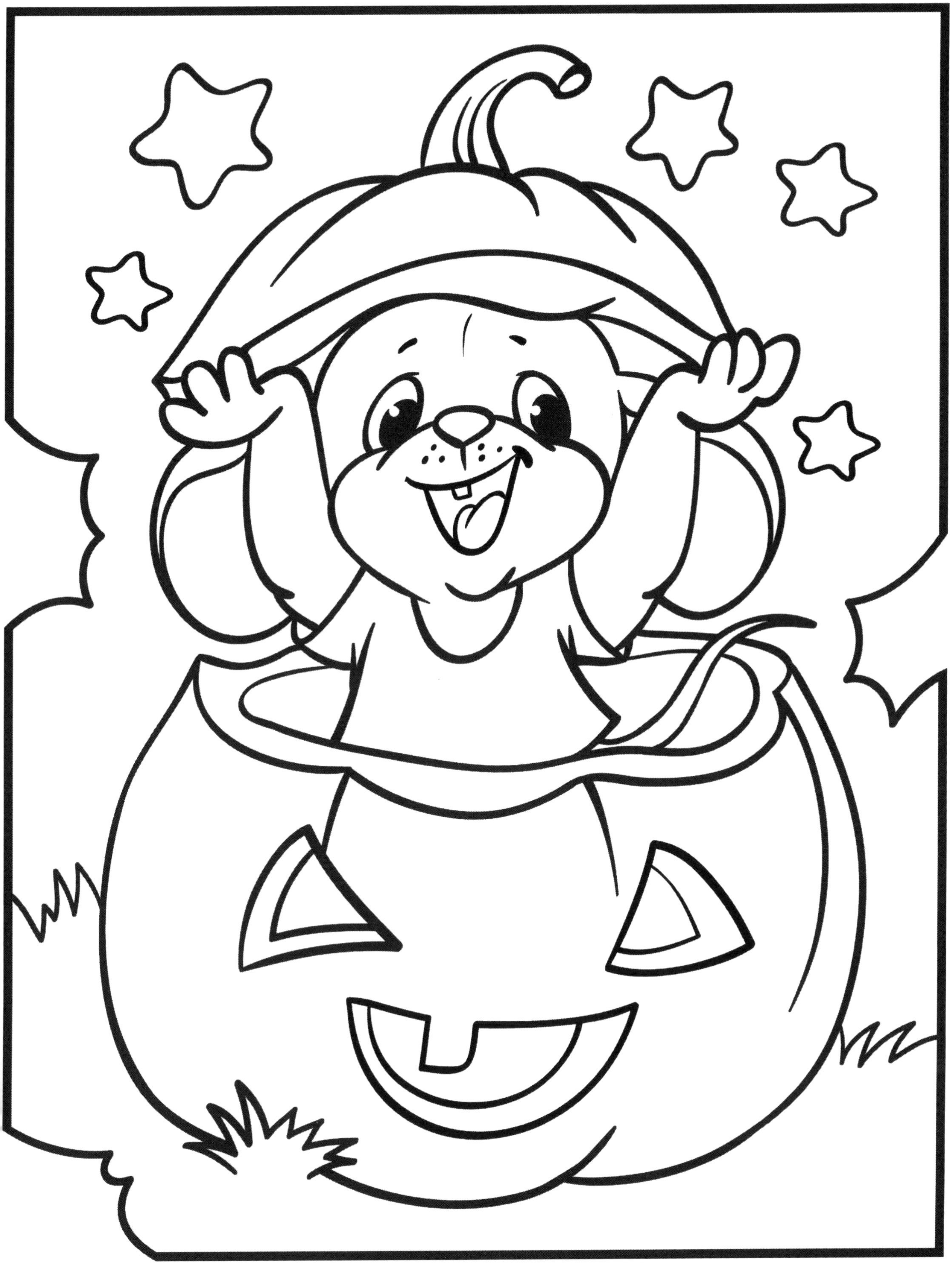

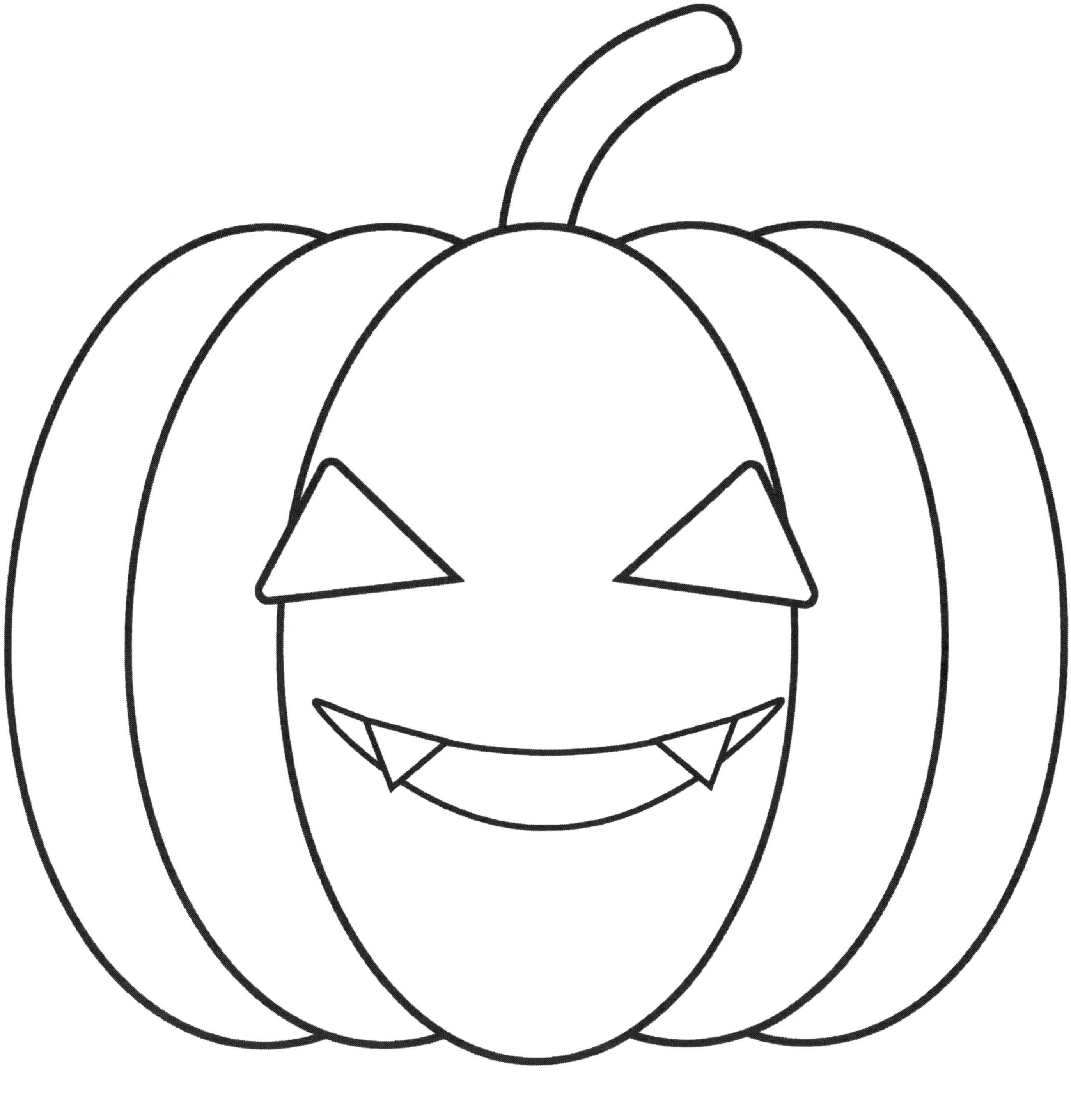

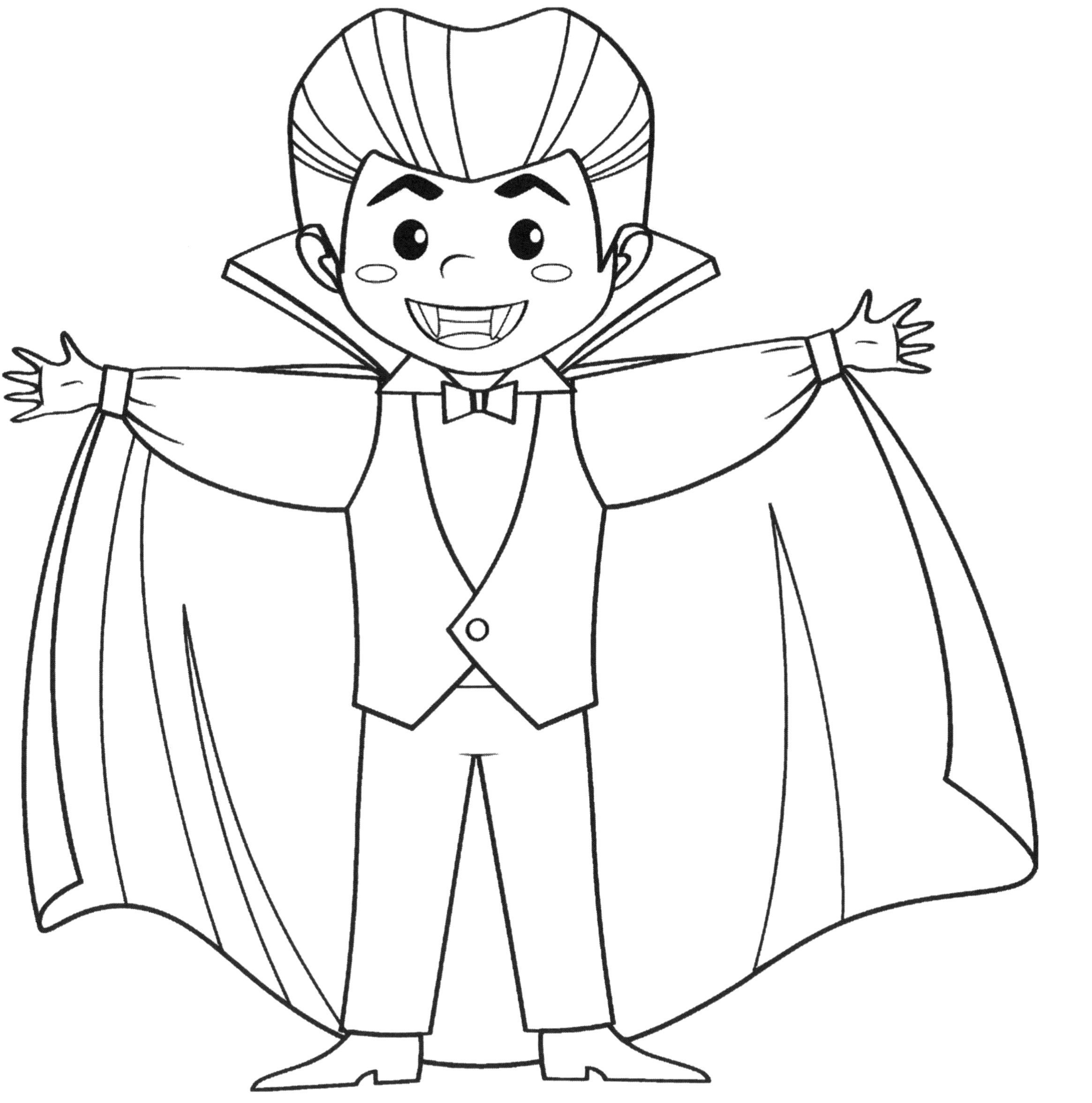

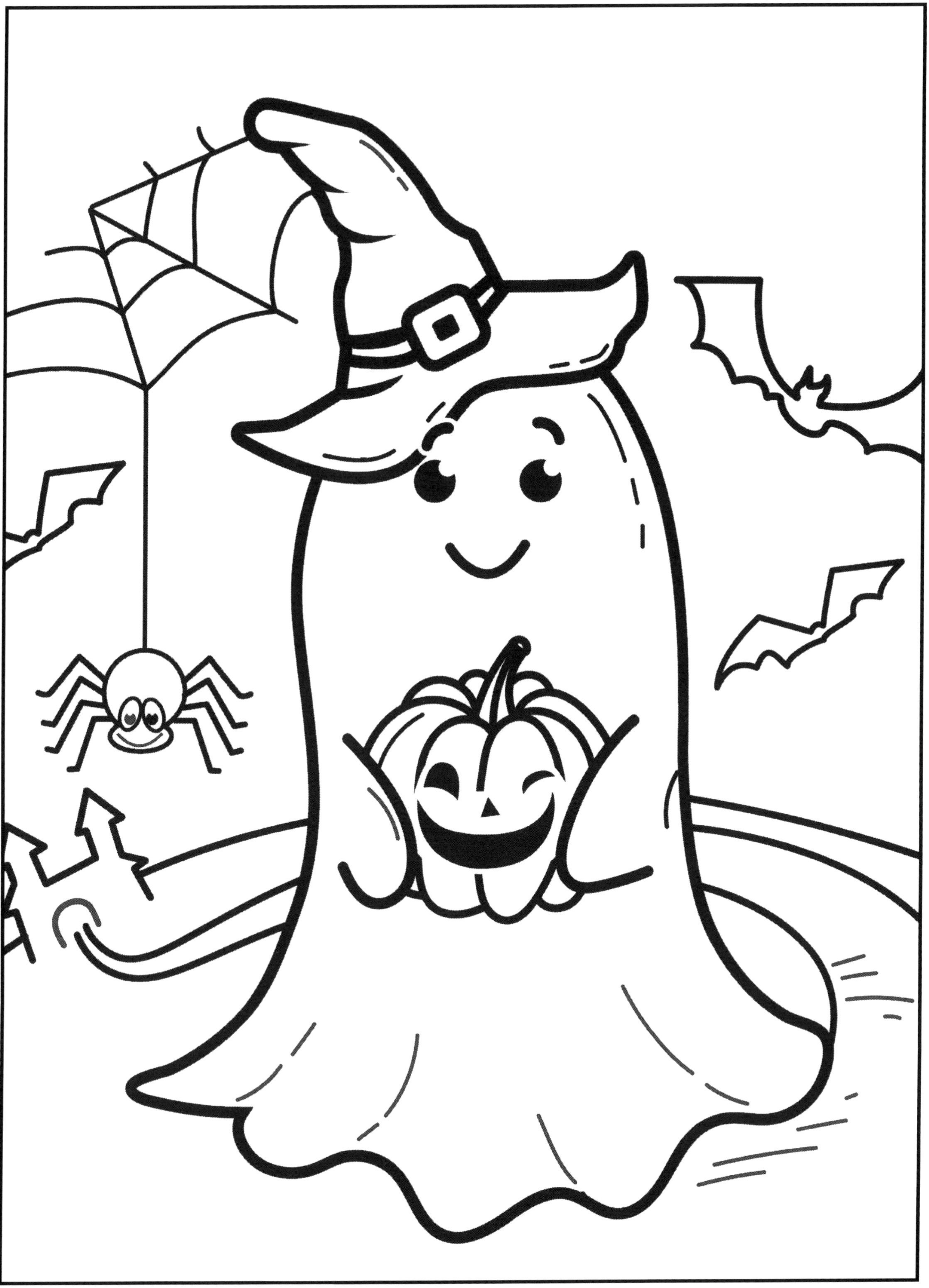

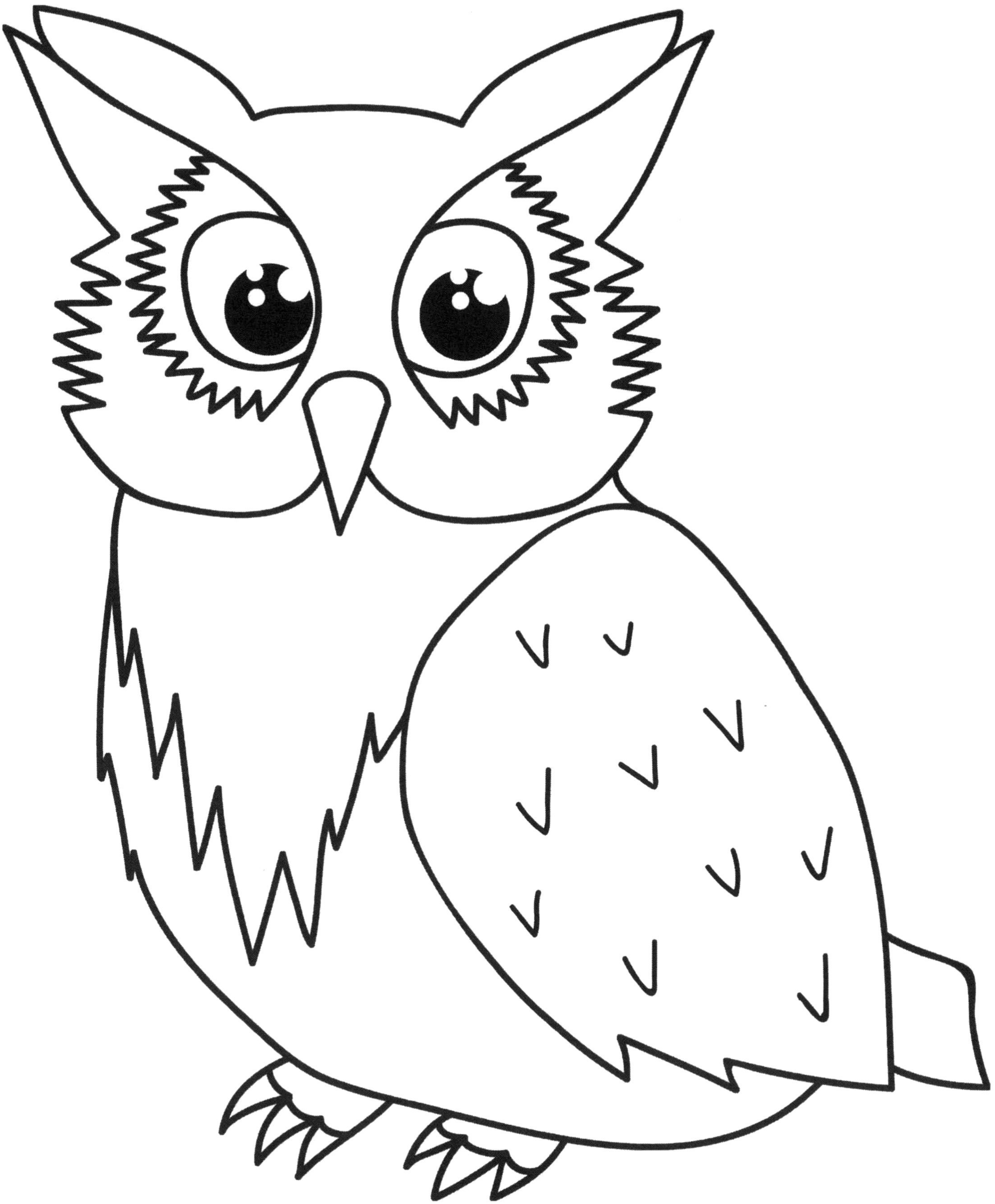

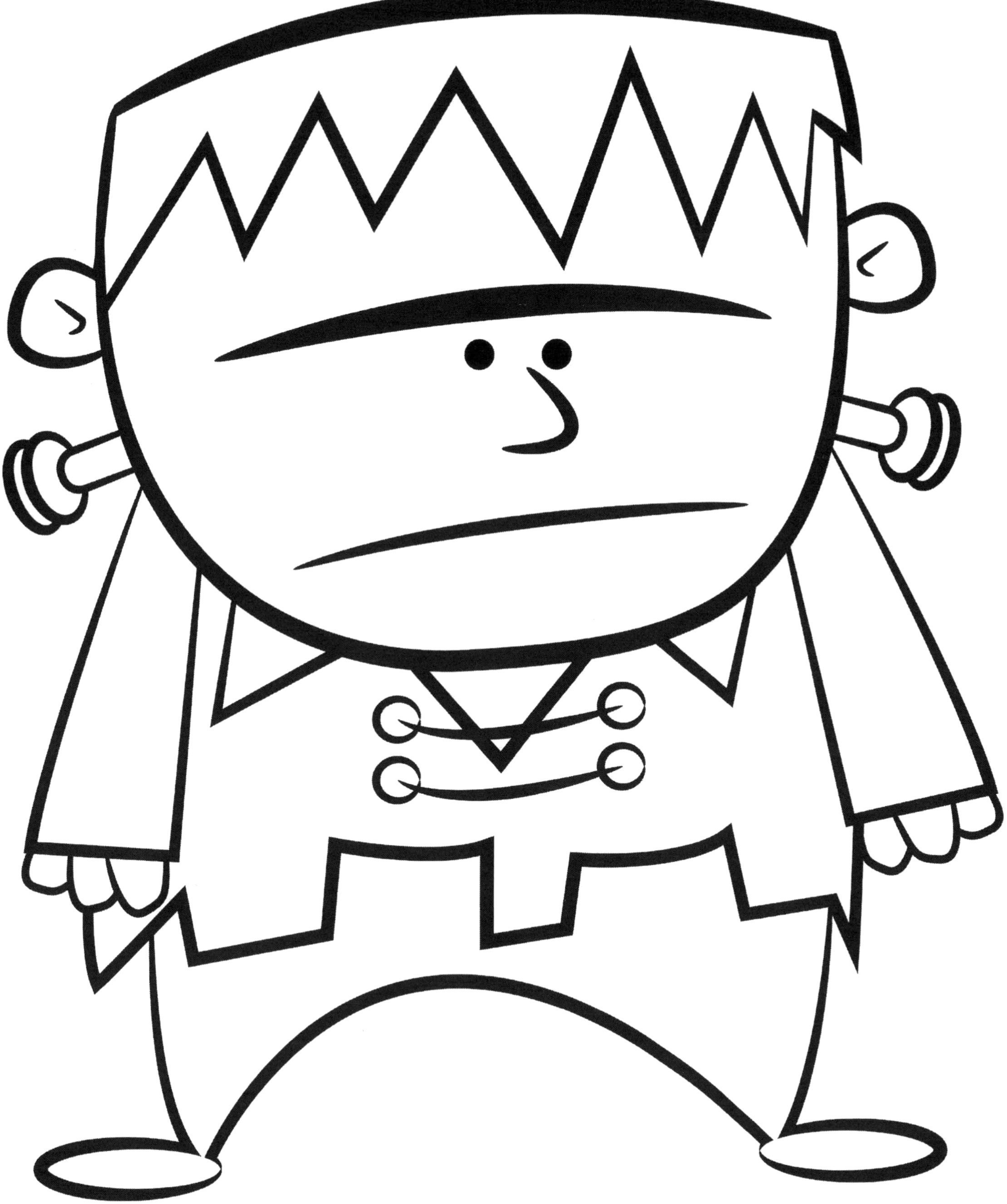

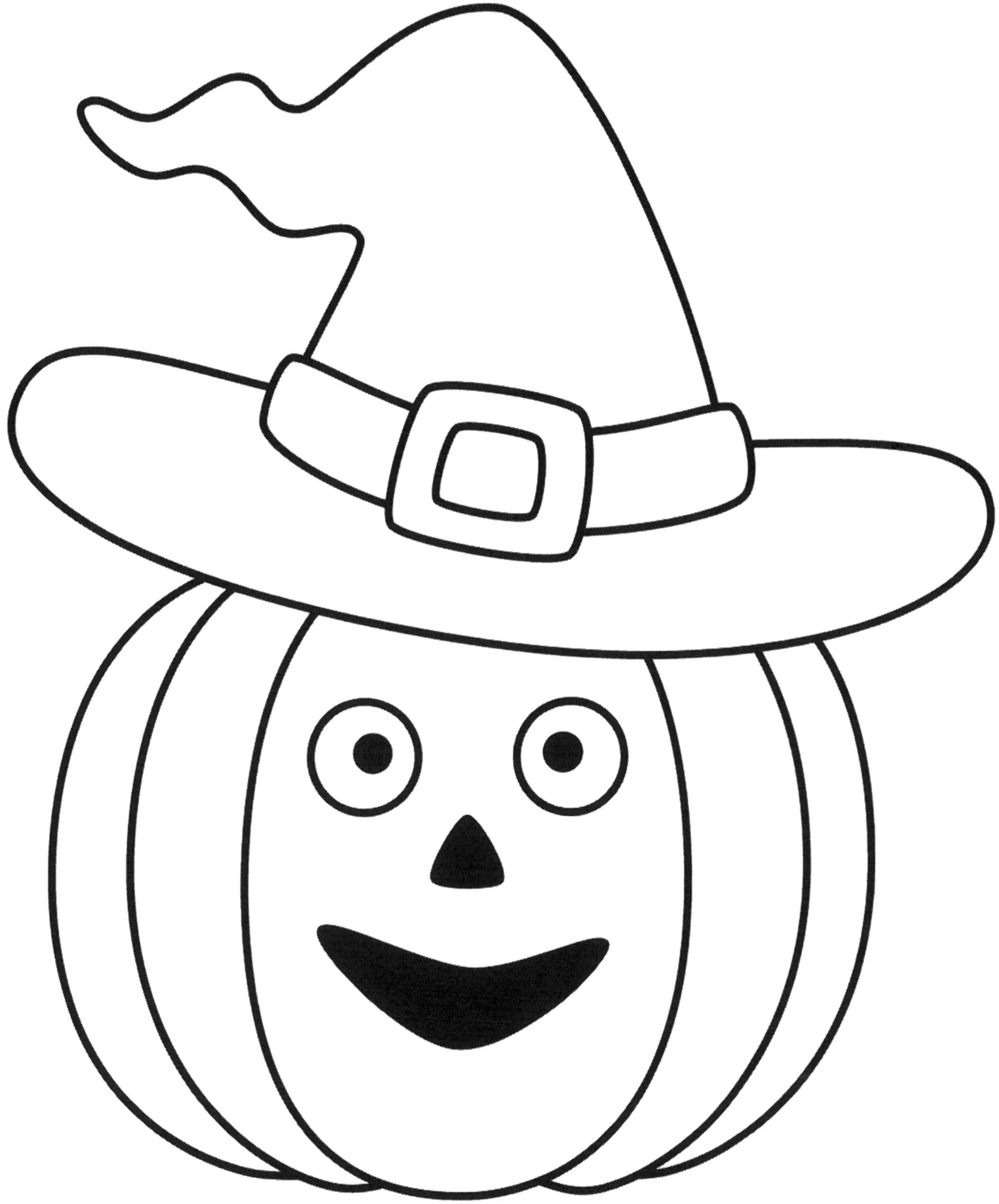

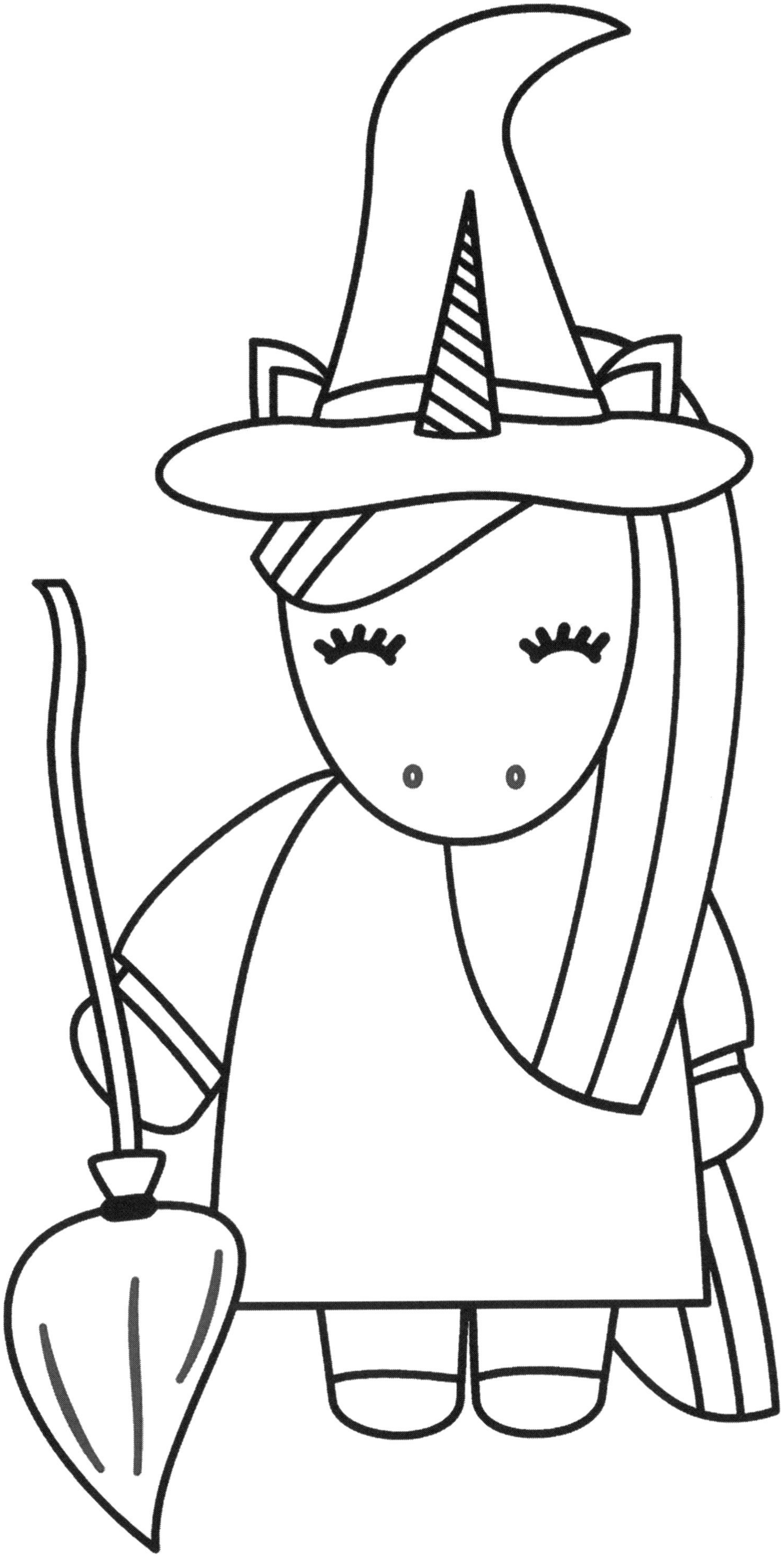

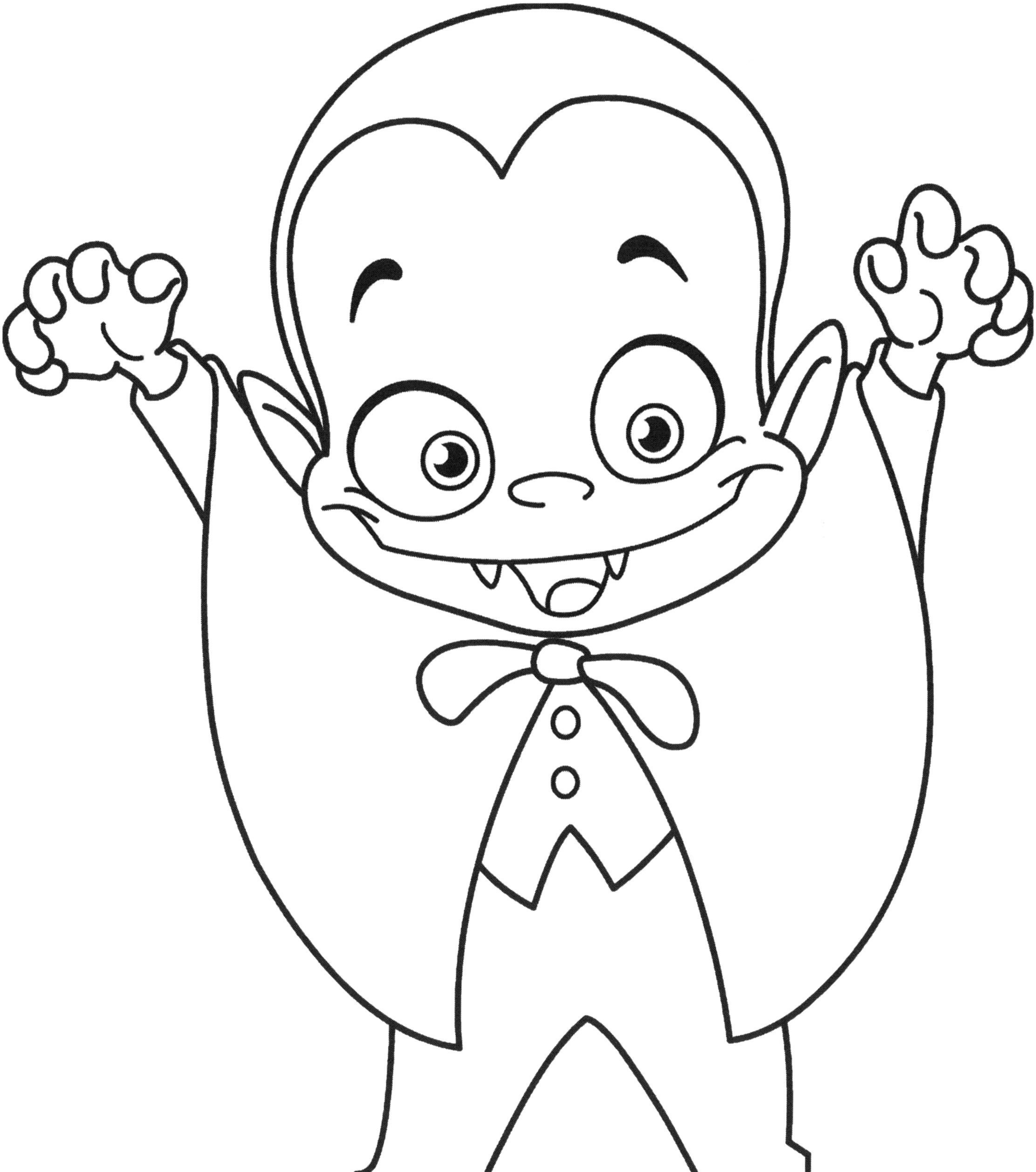

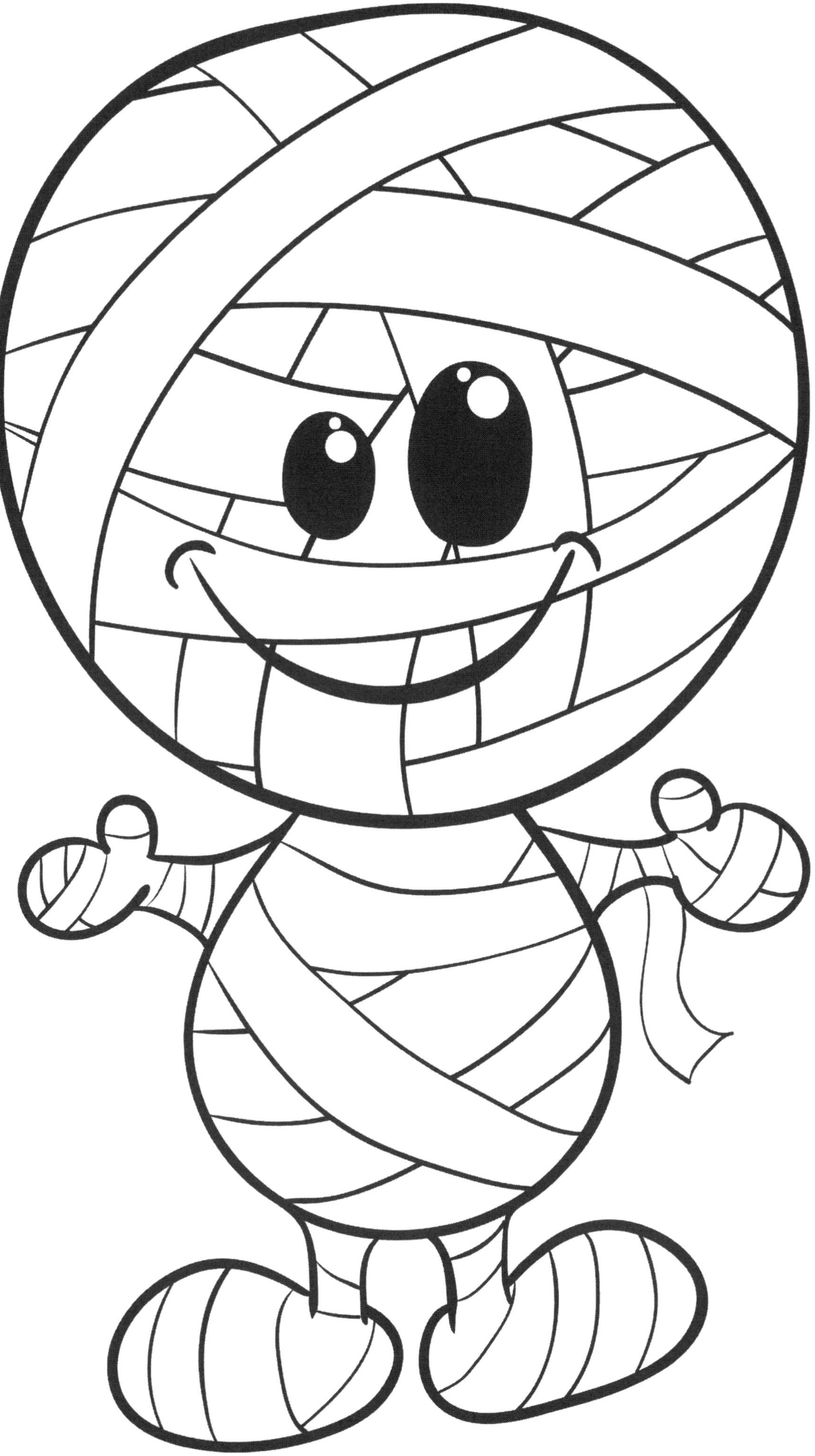

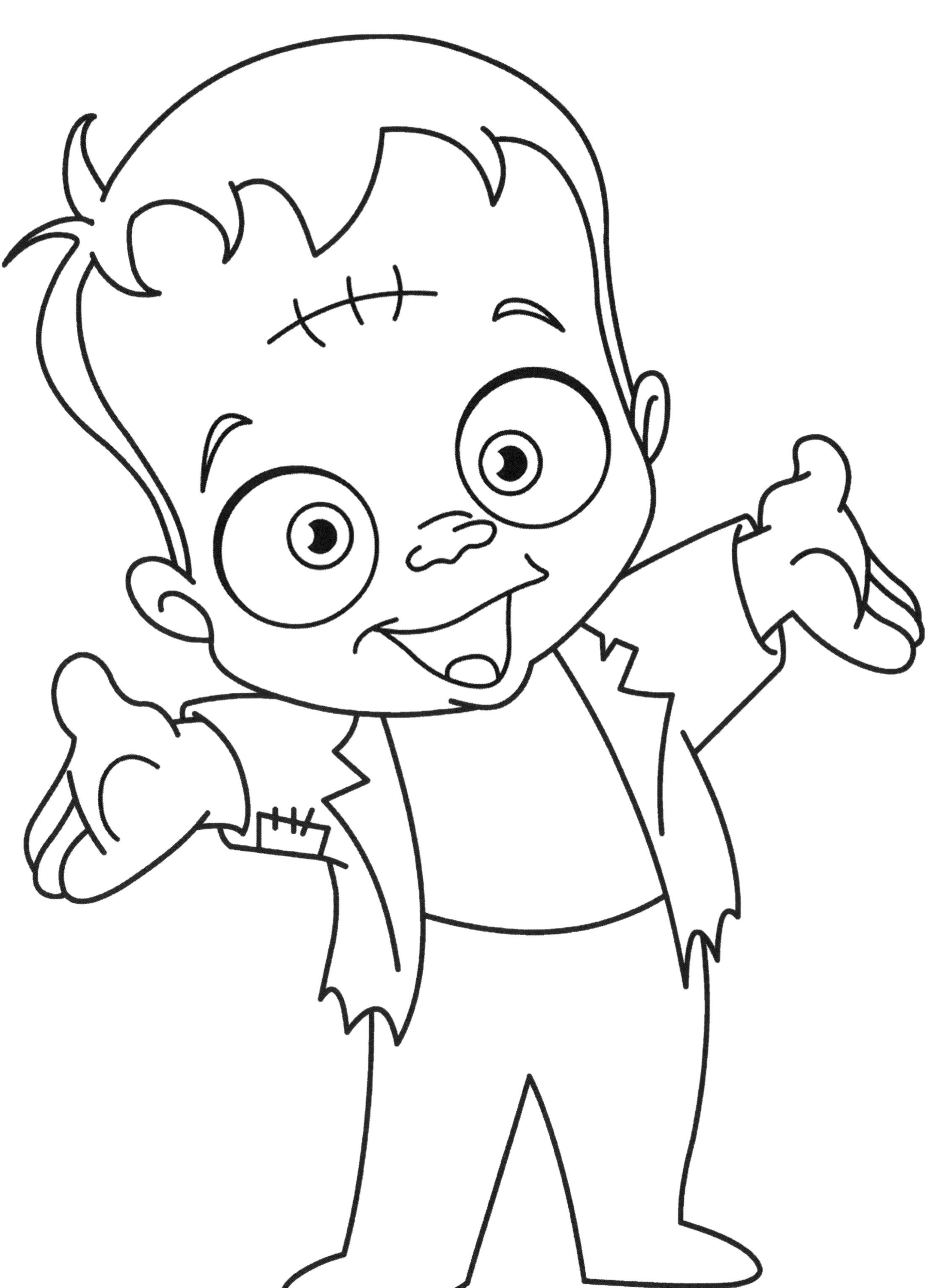

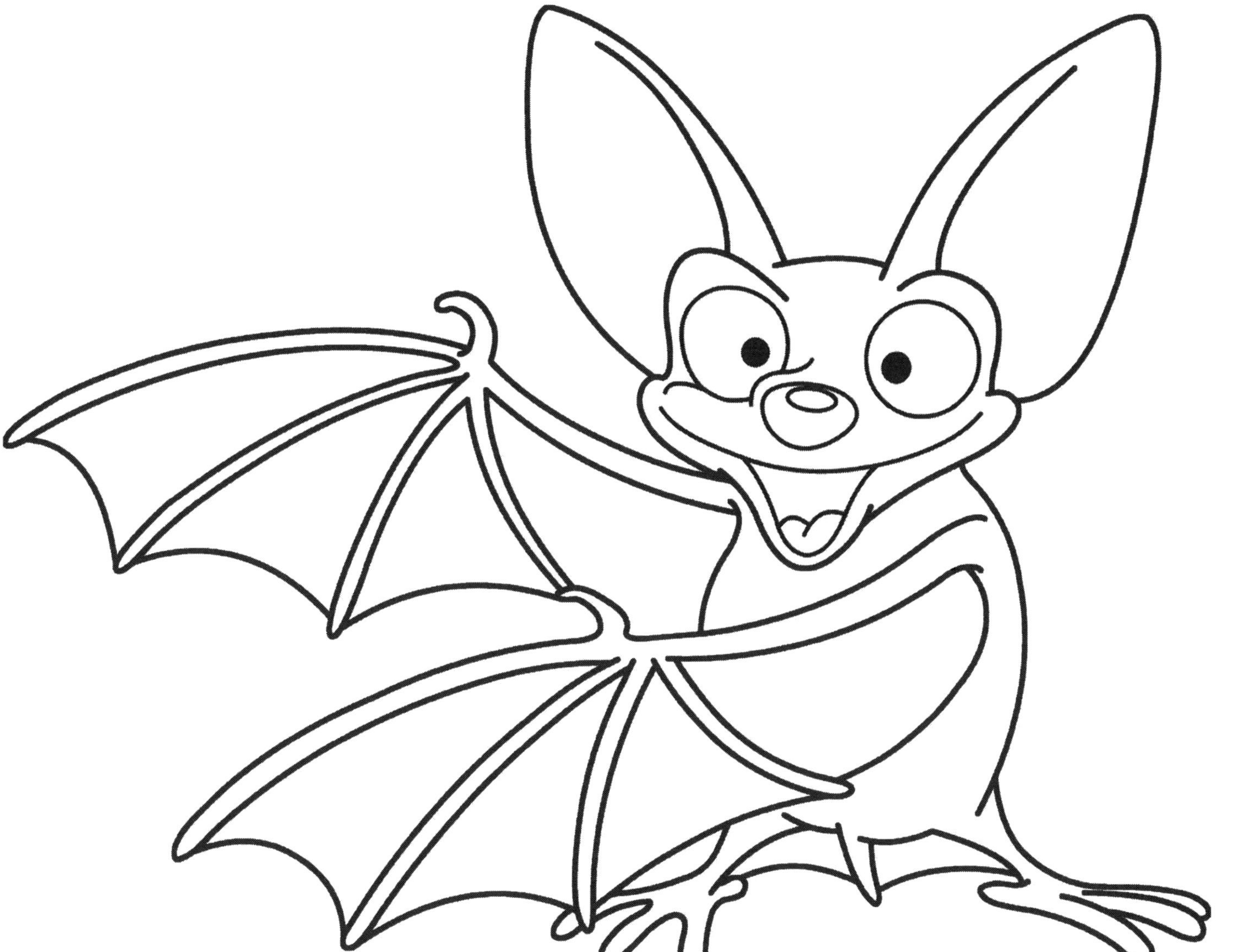

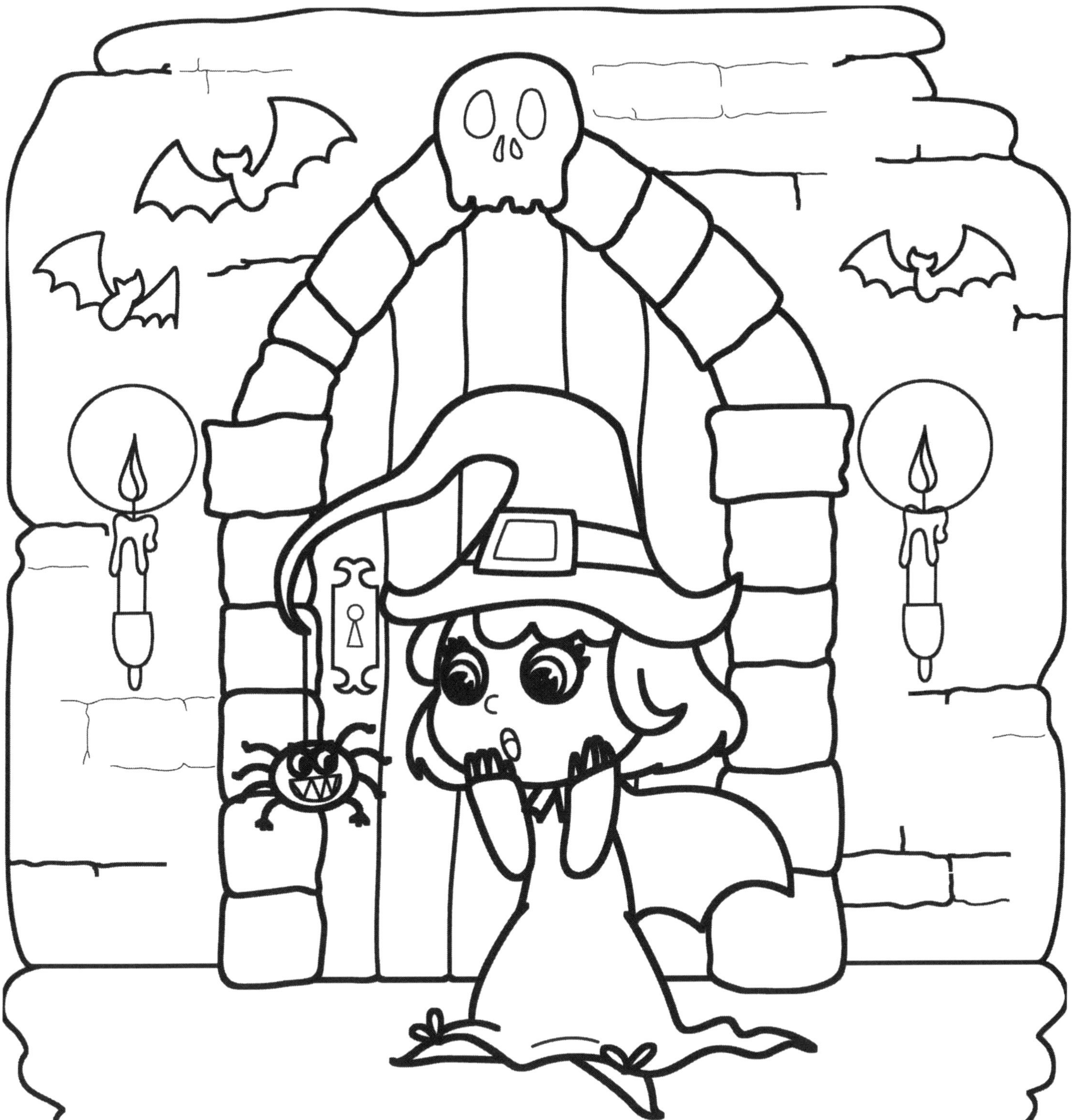

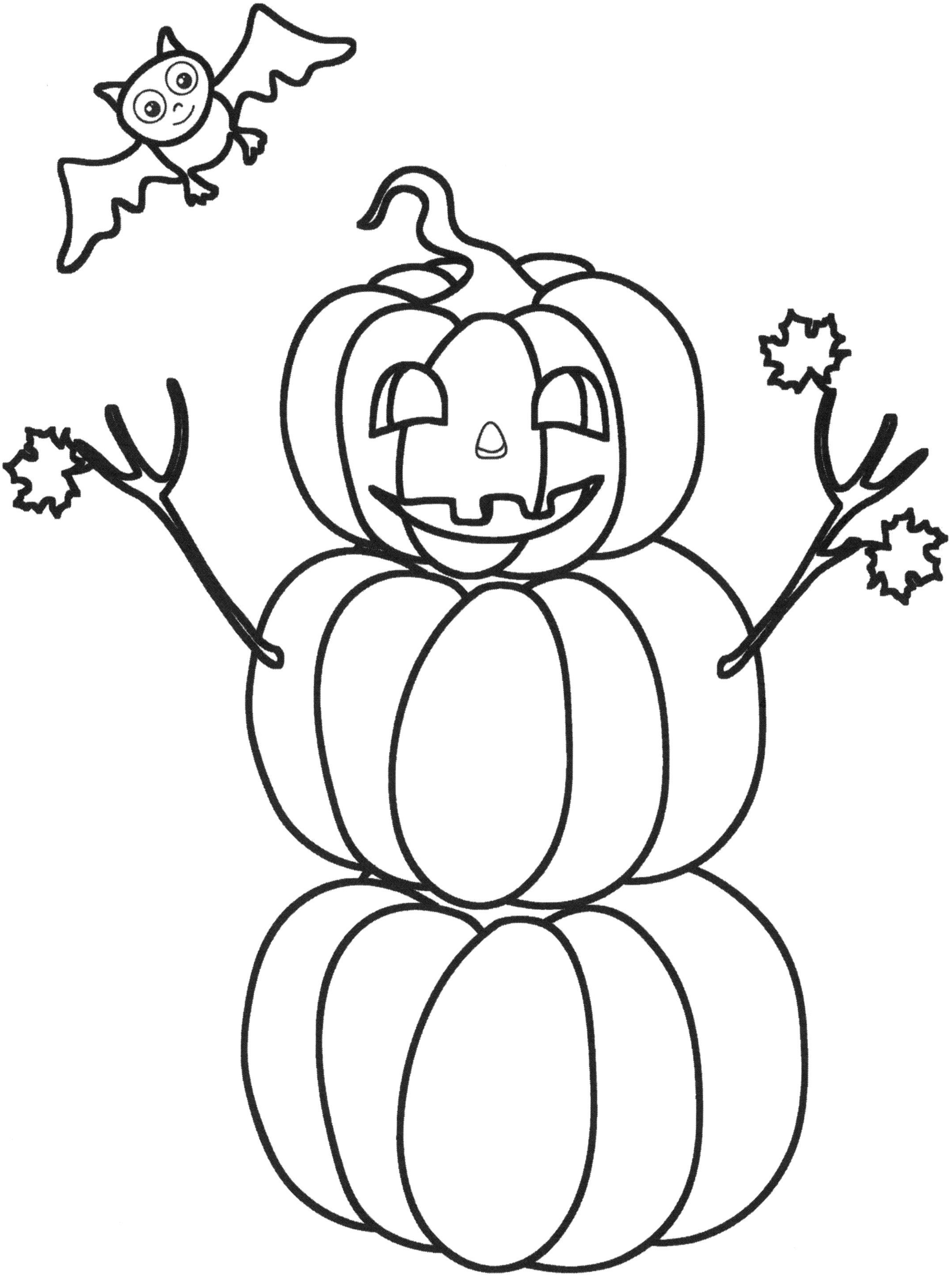

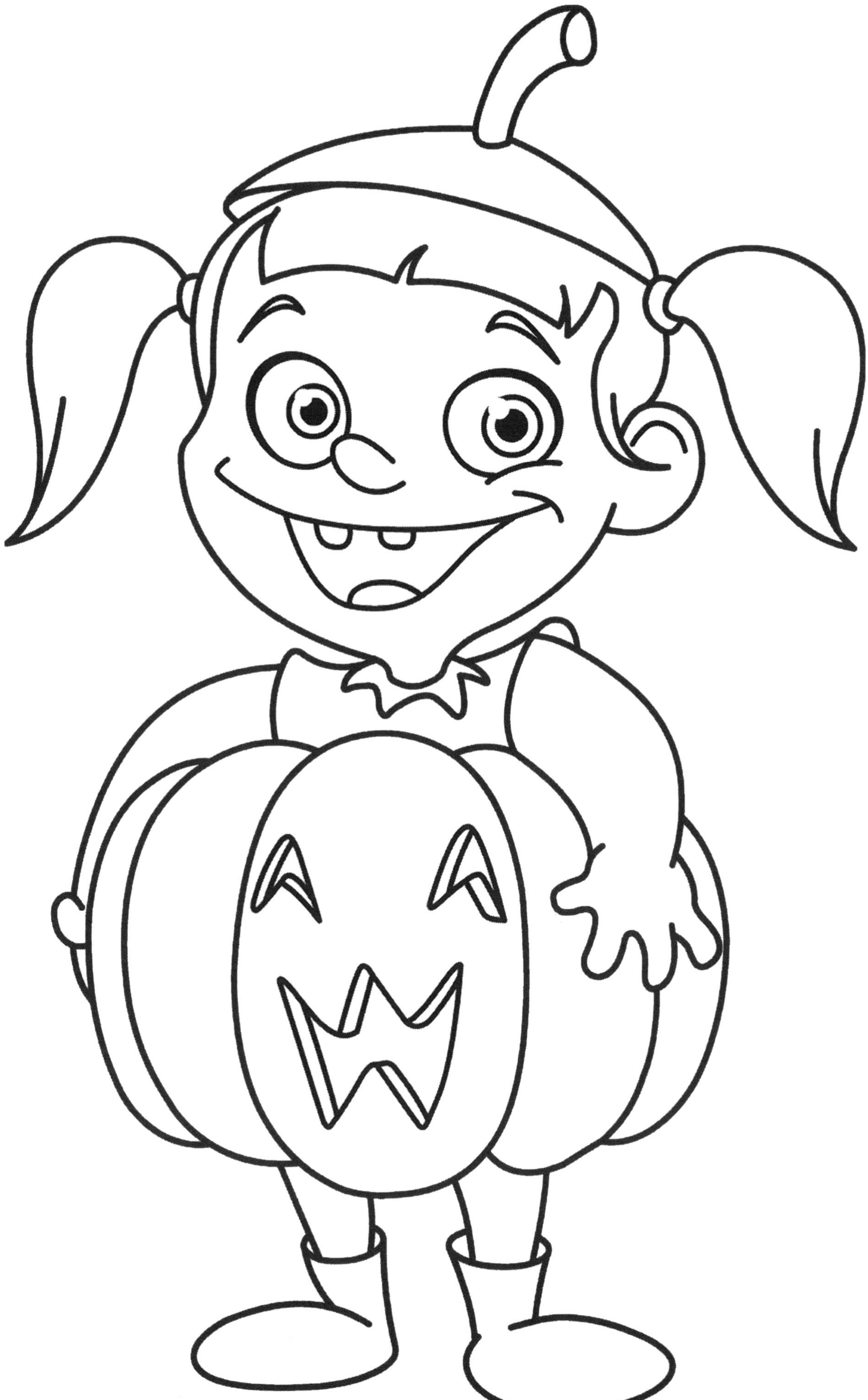

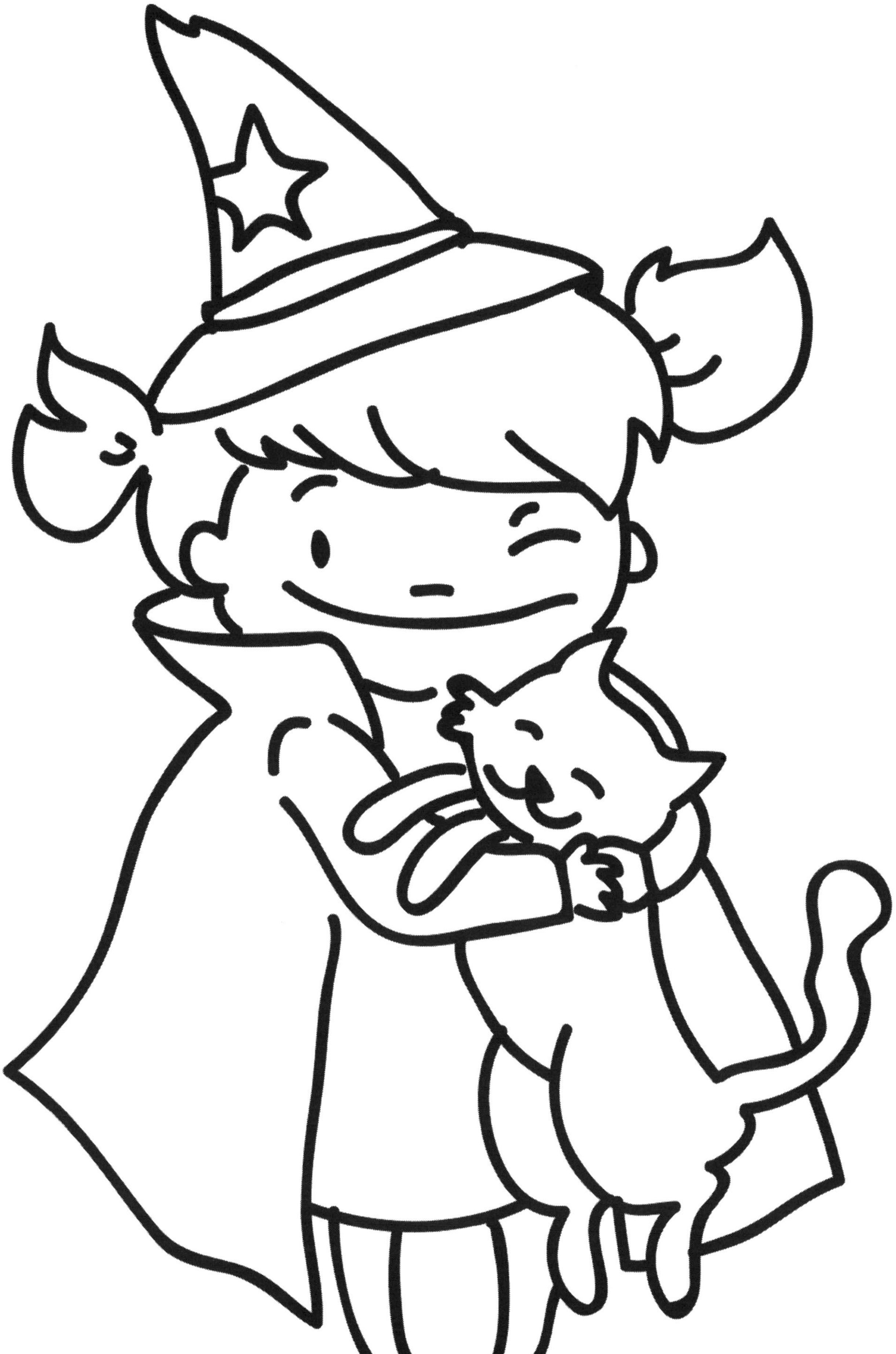

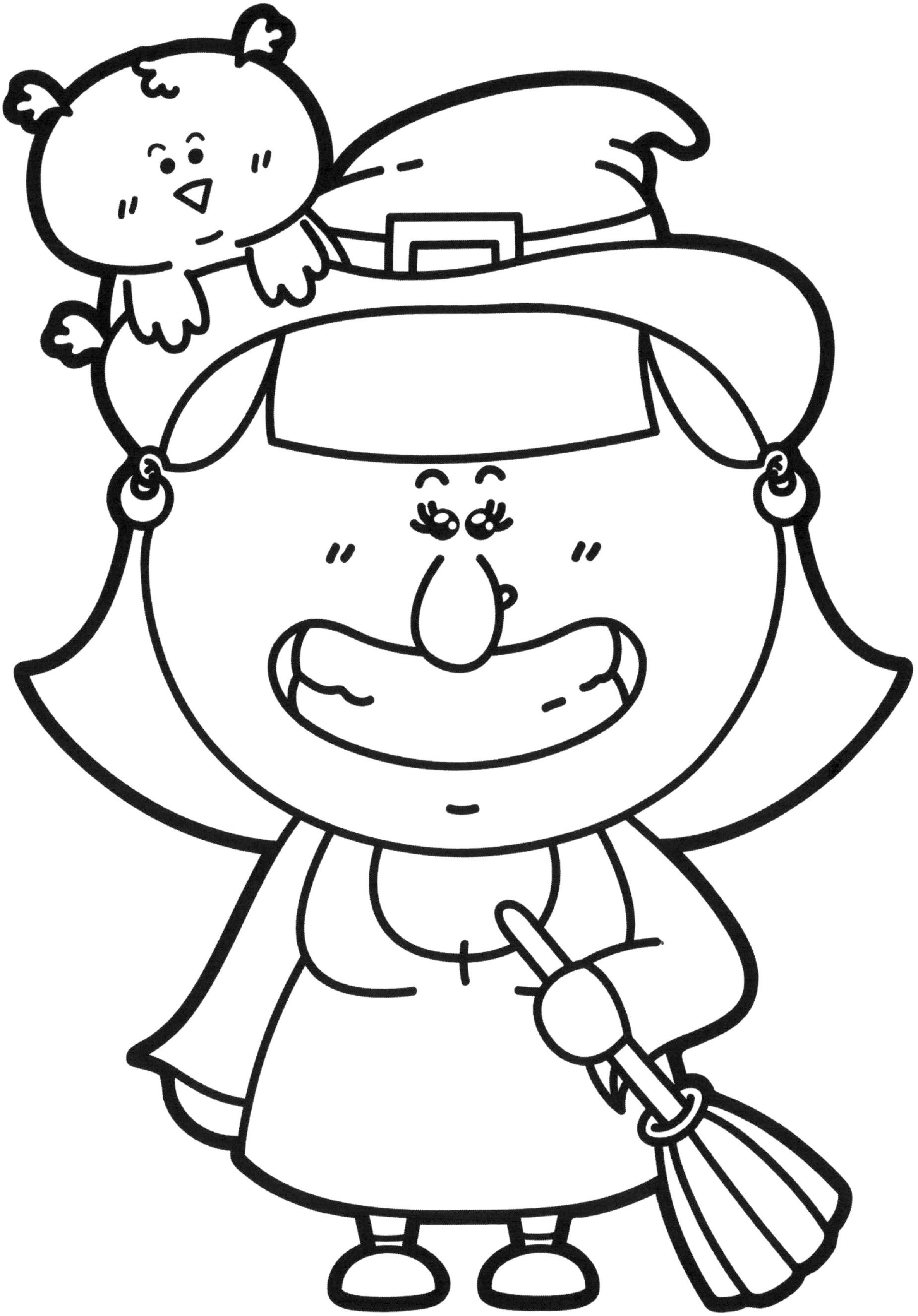

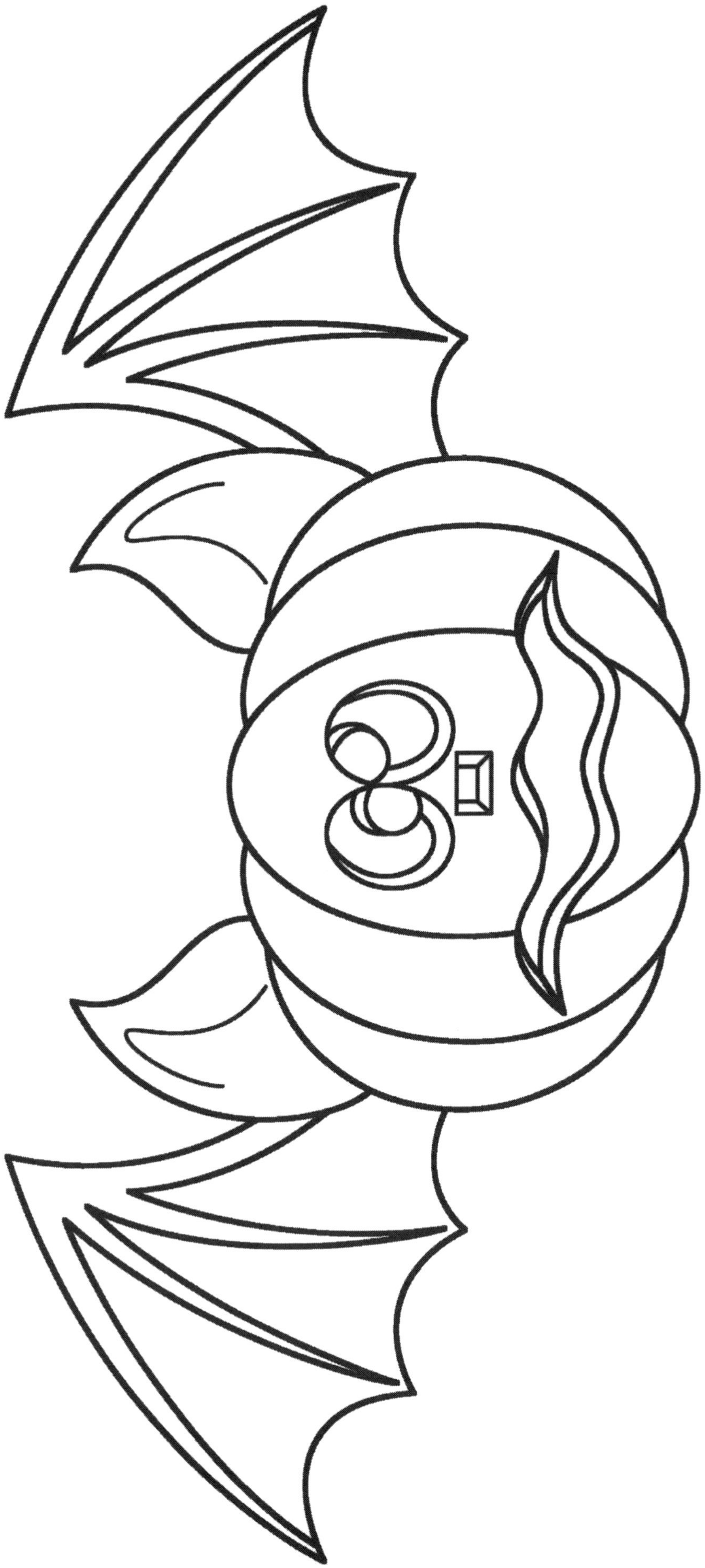

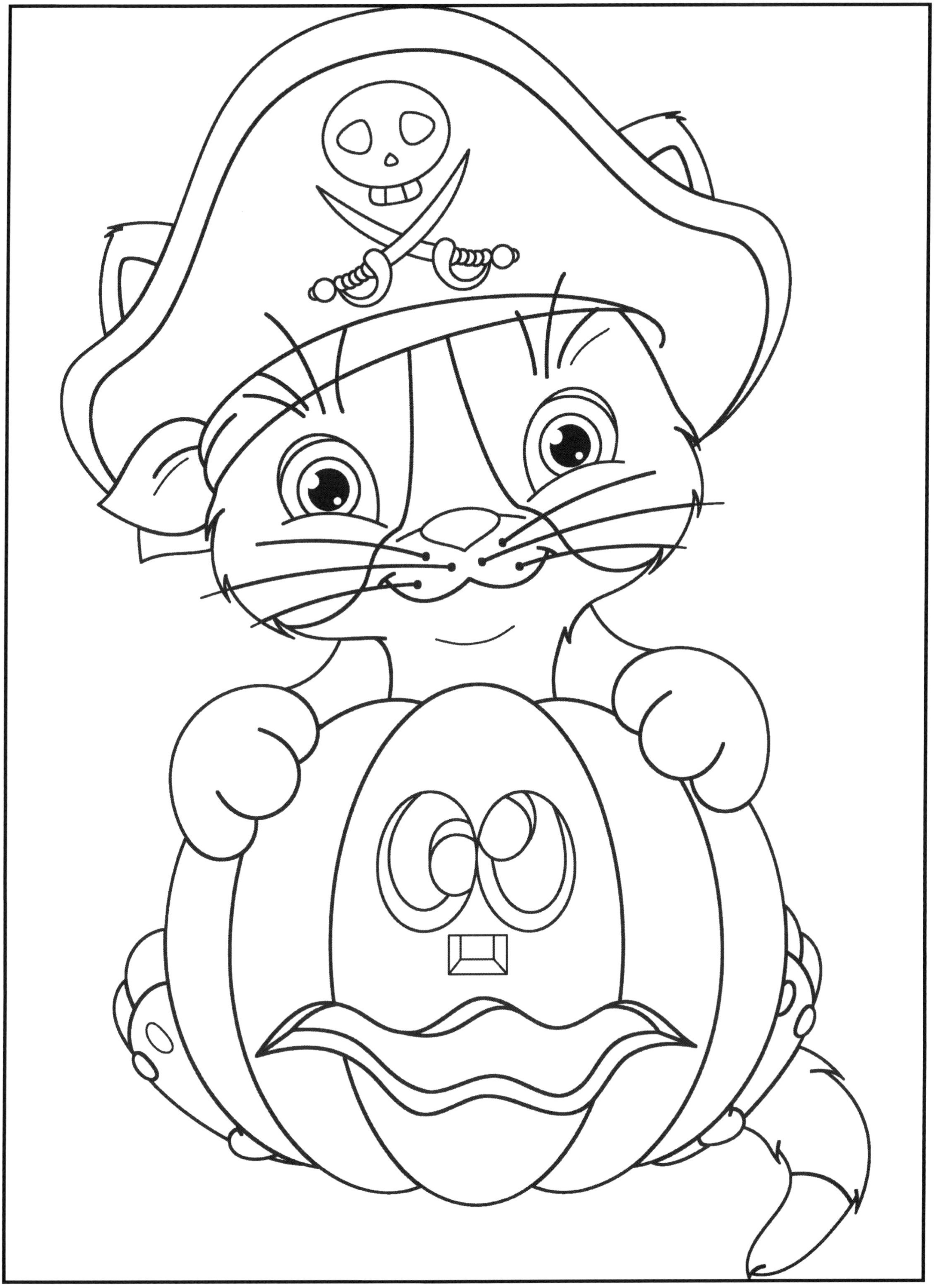

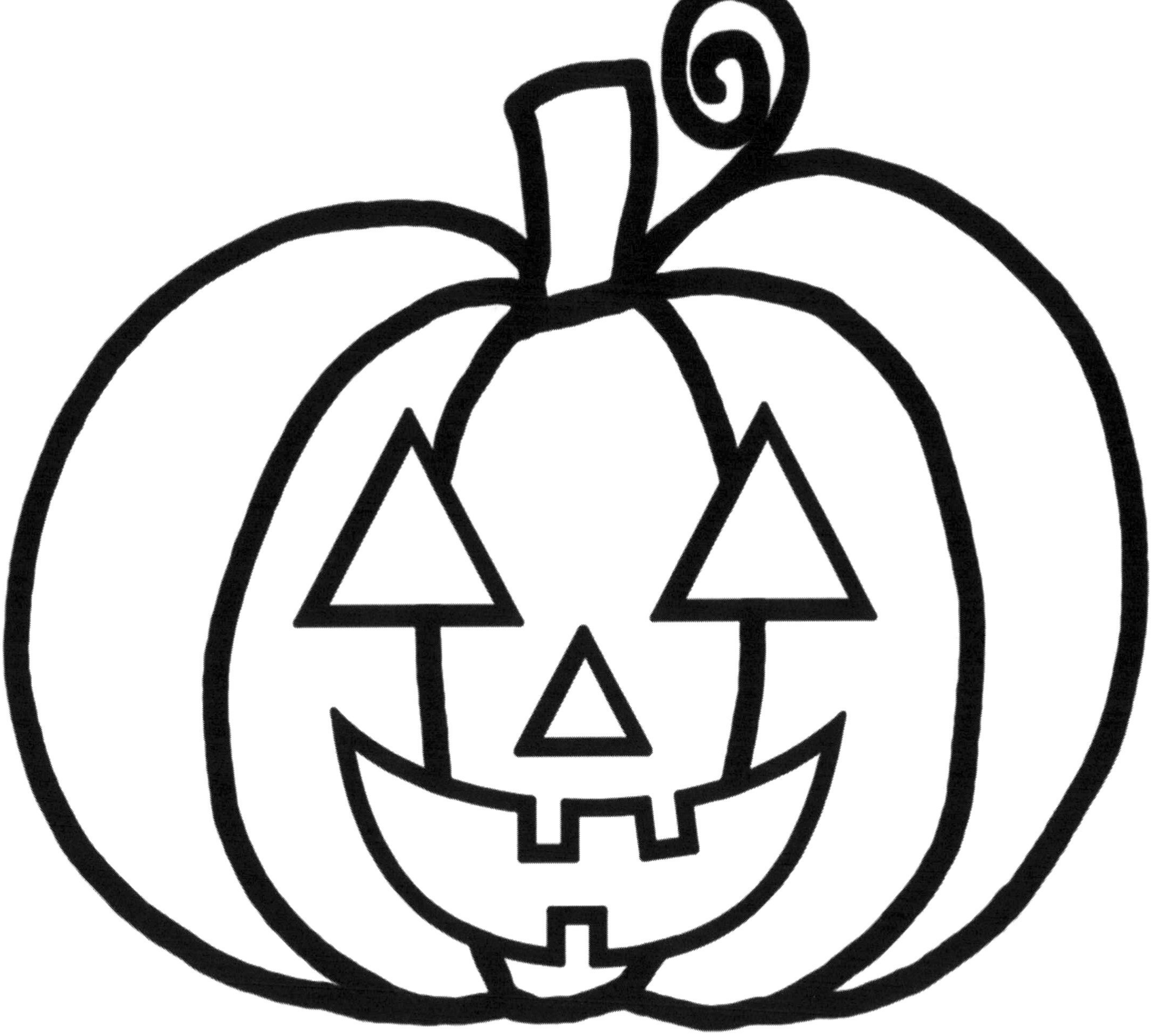

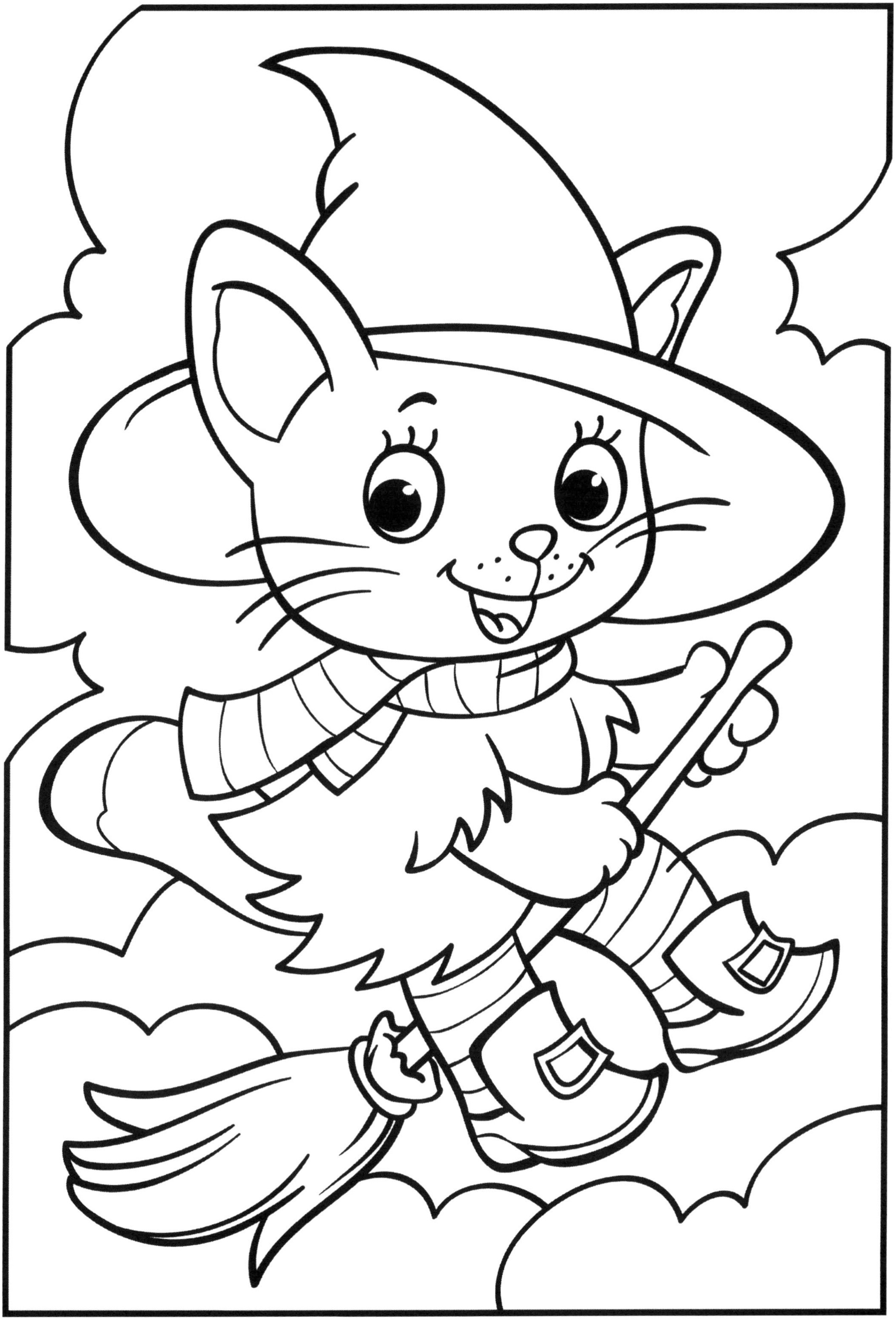

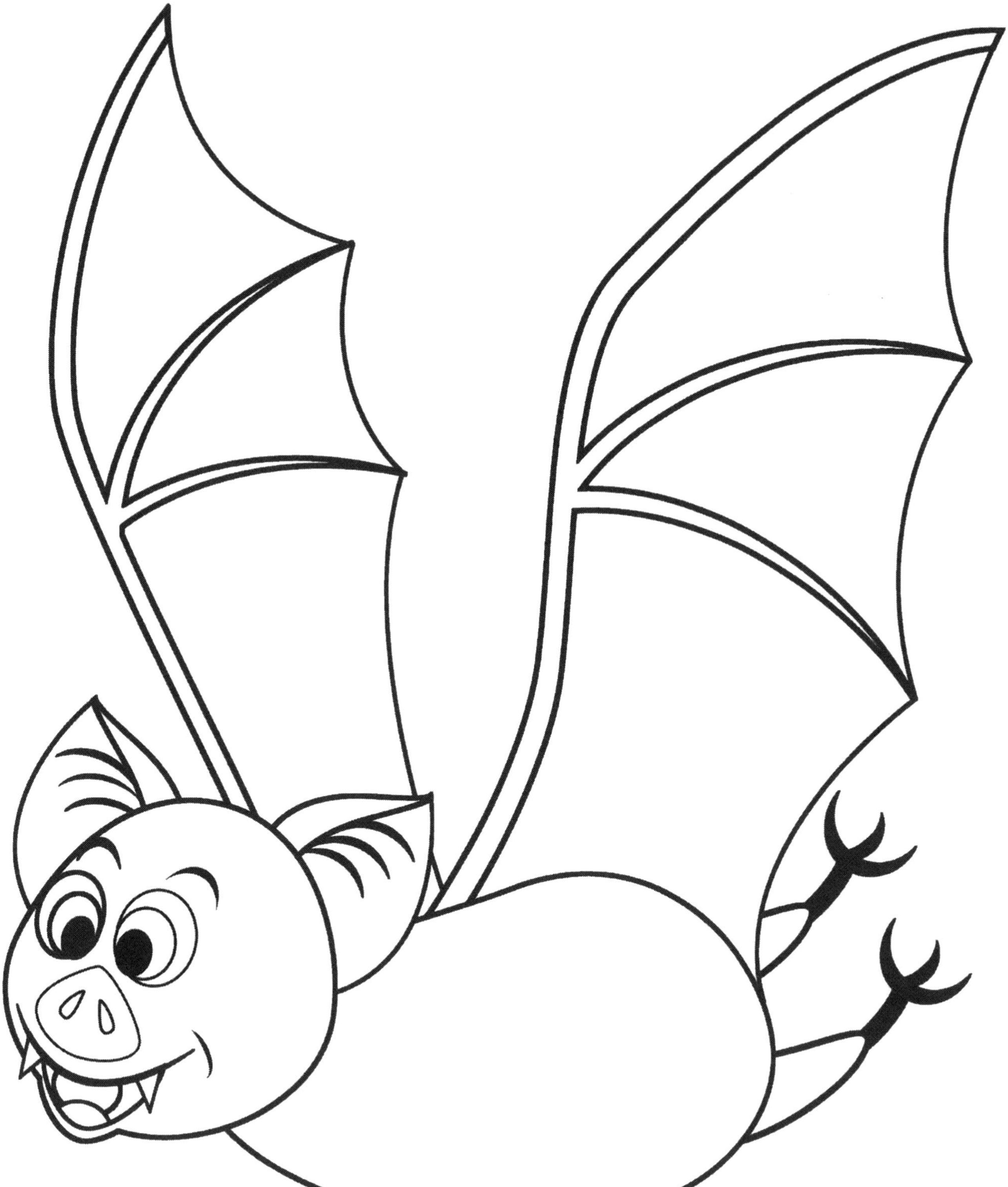

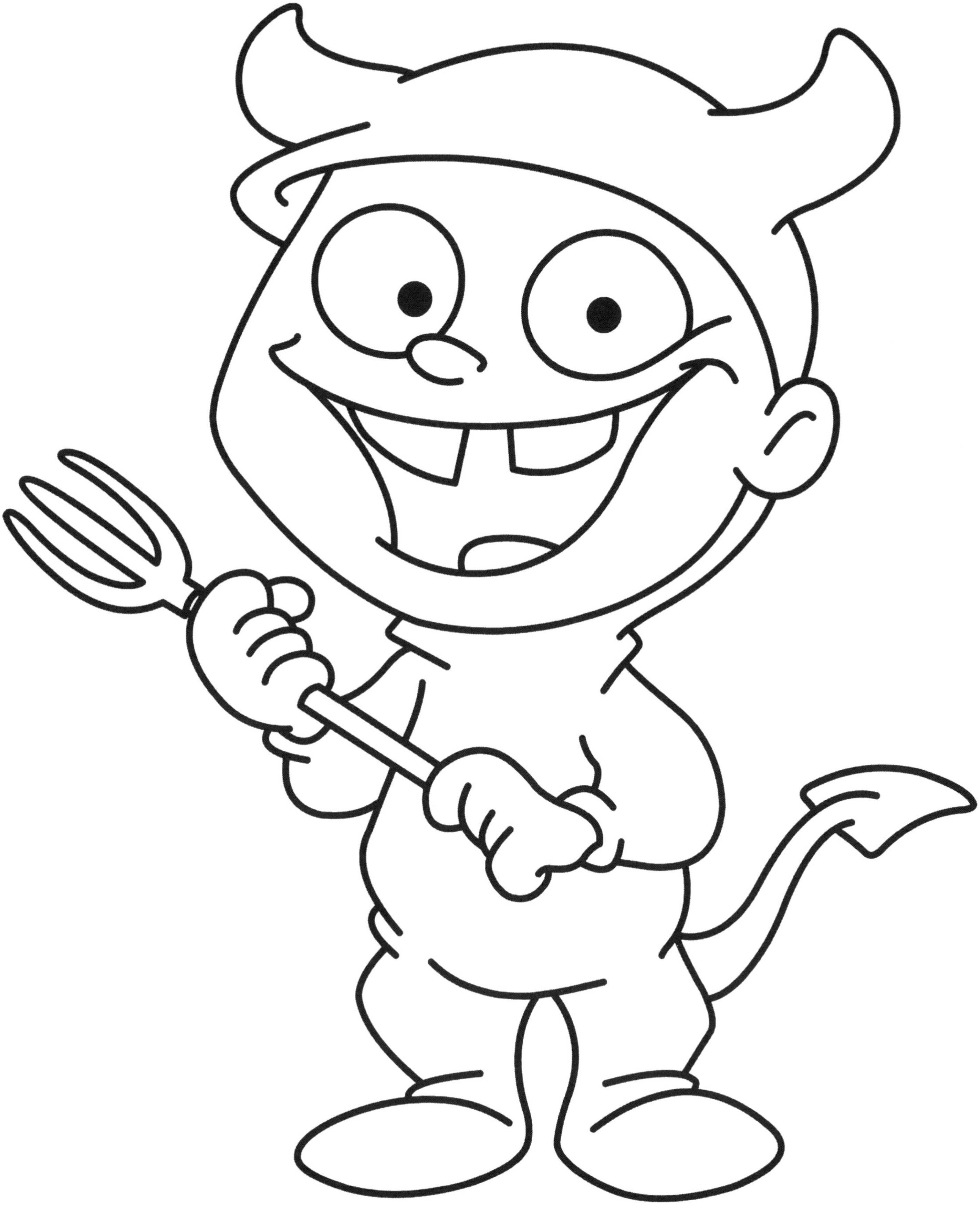

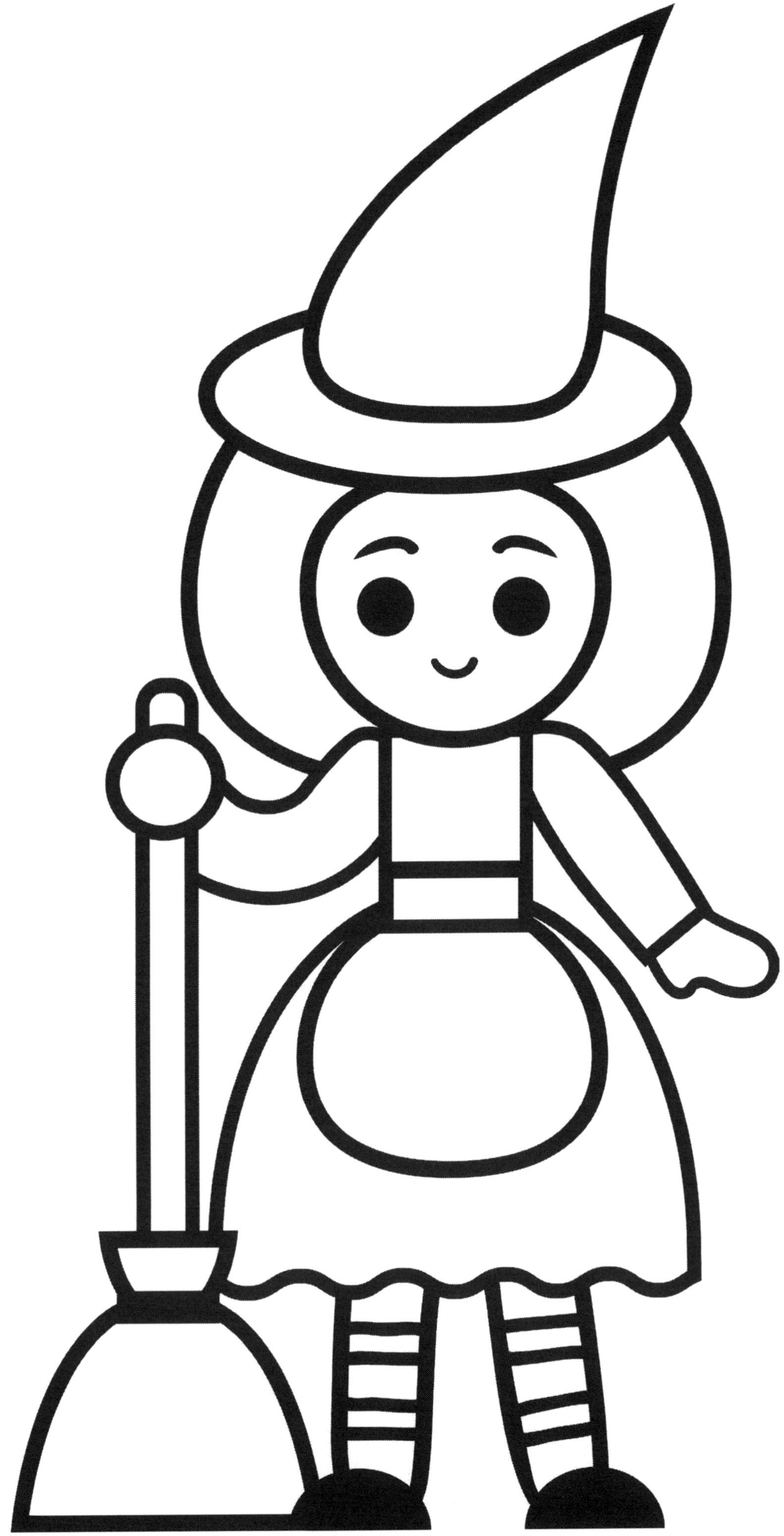

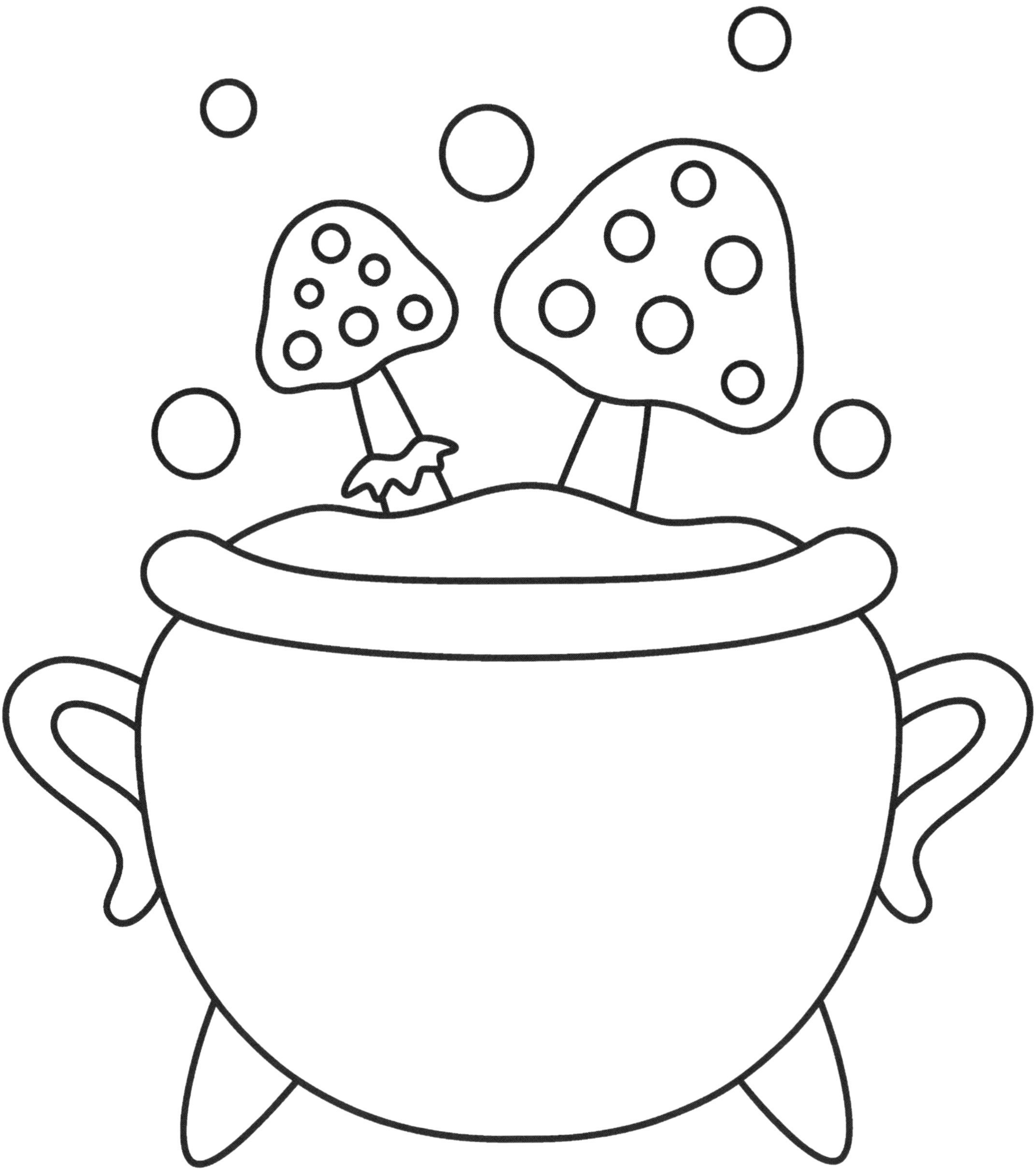

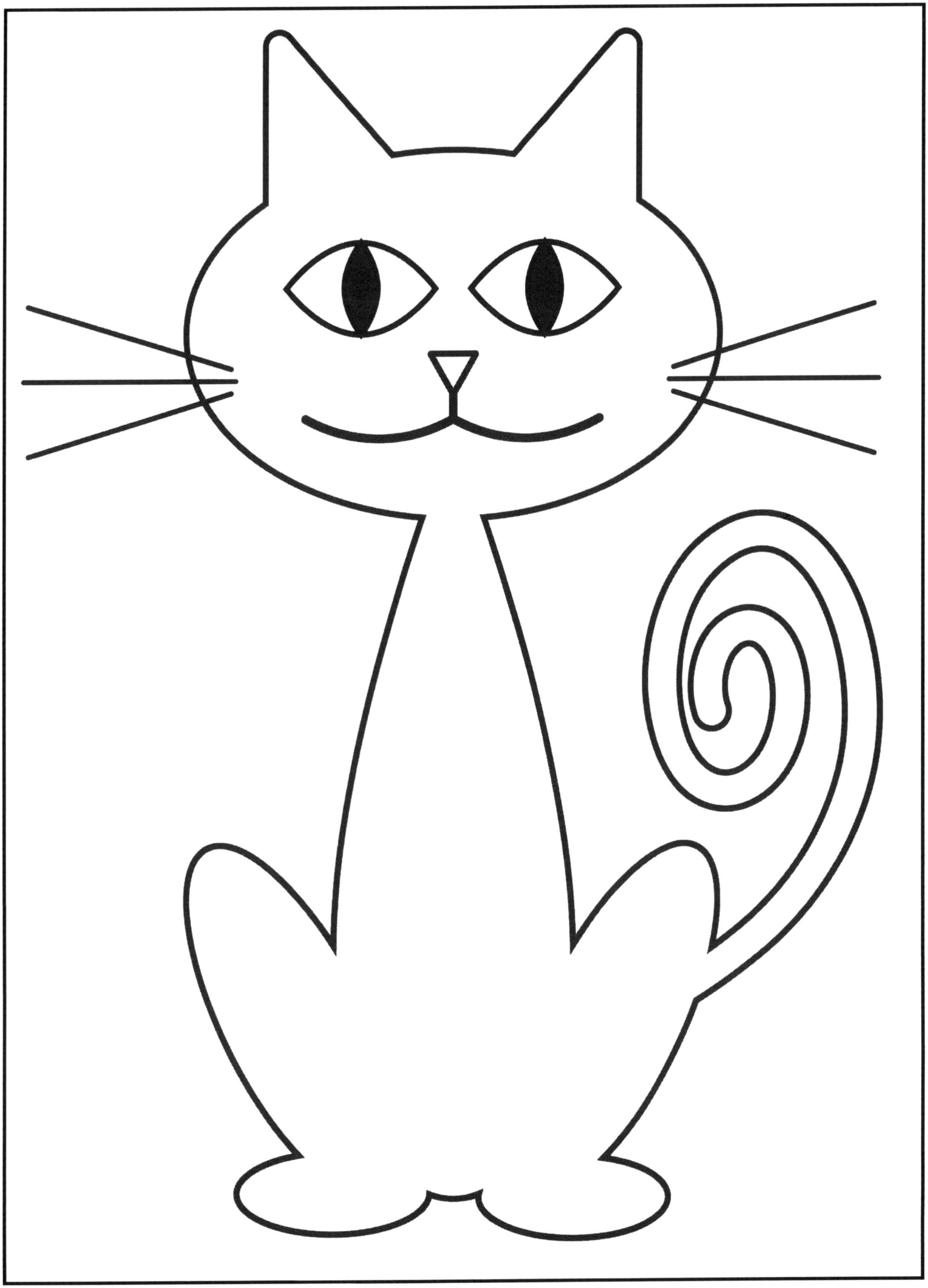

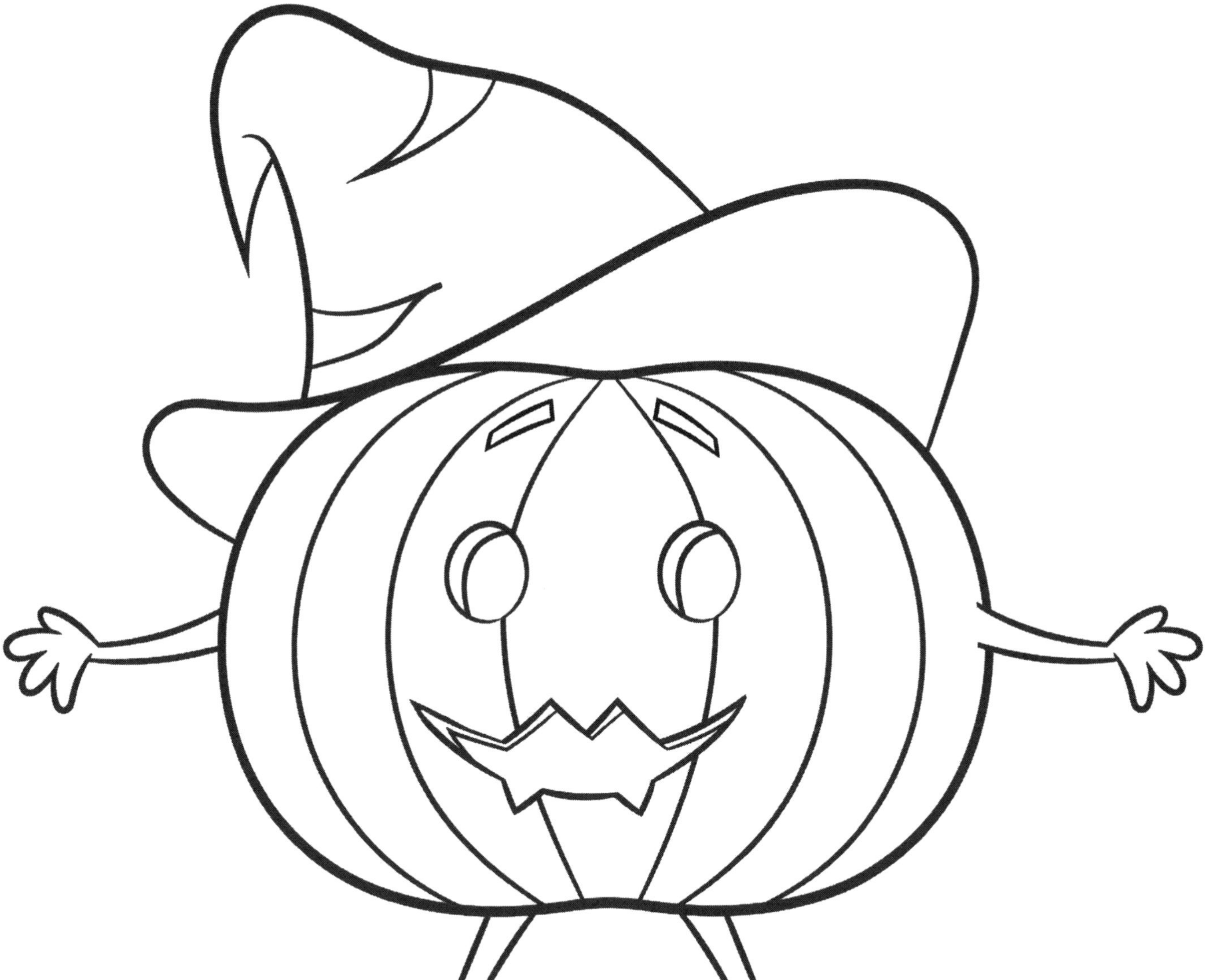

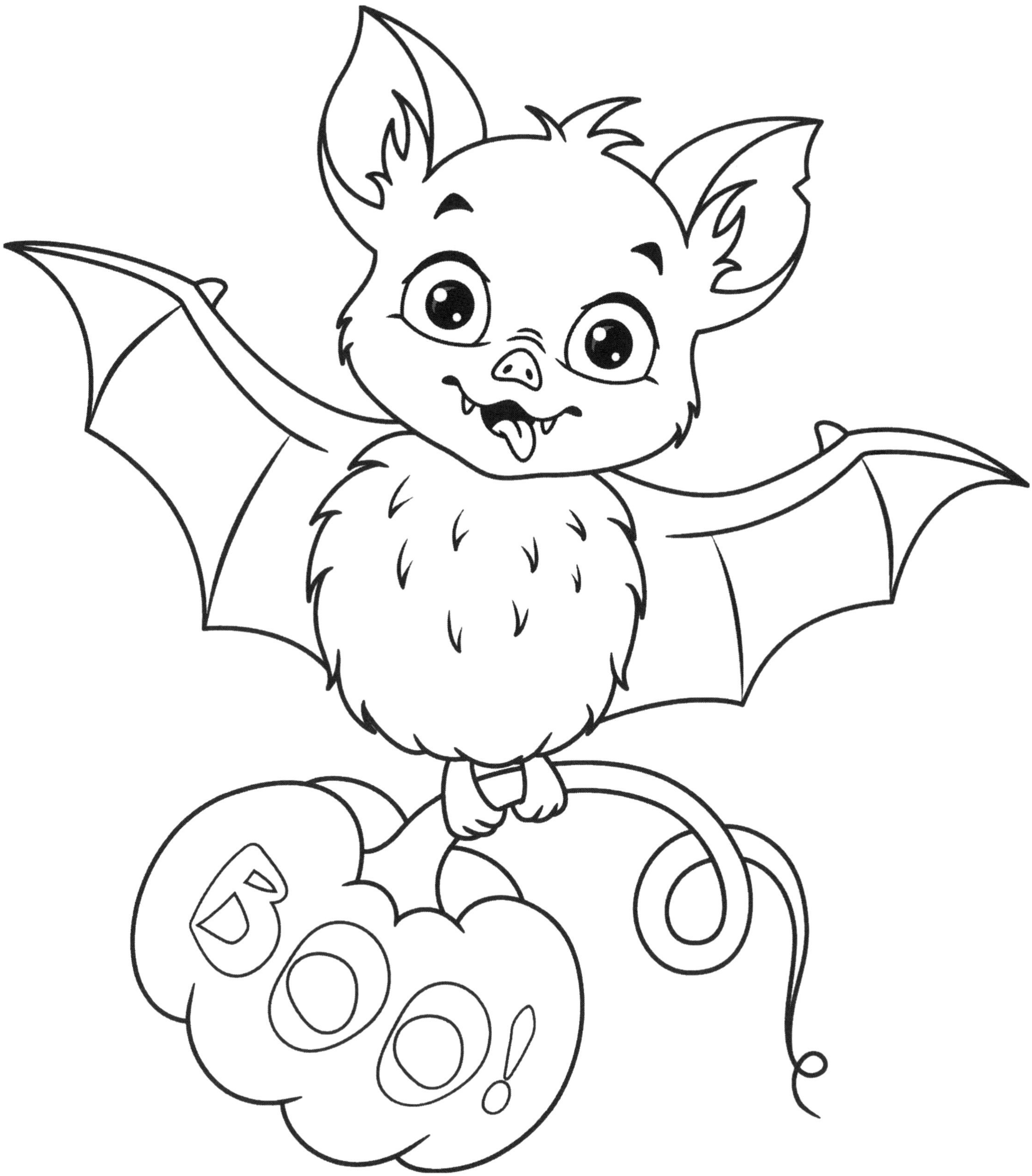
BOO!

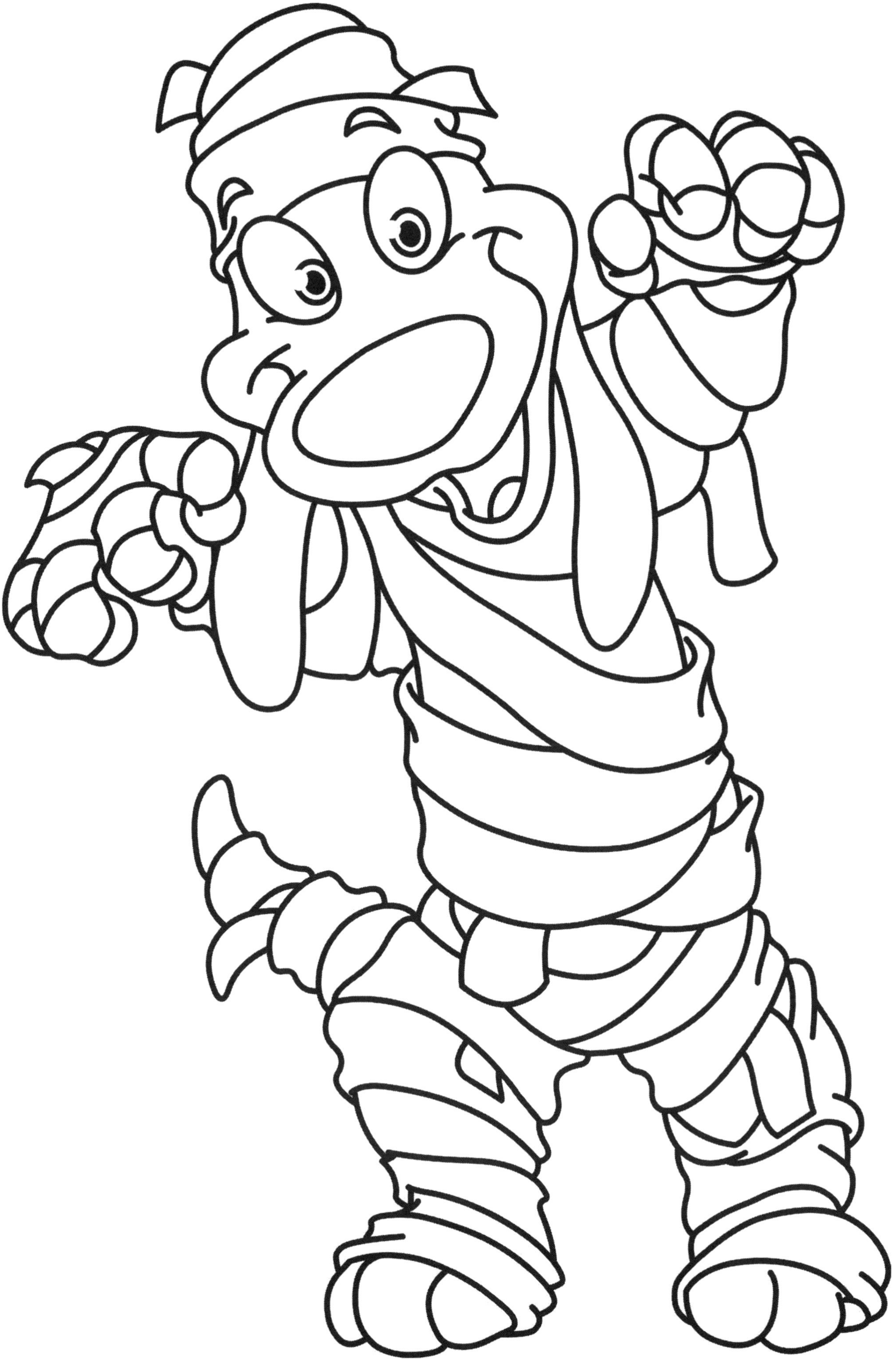

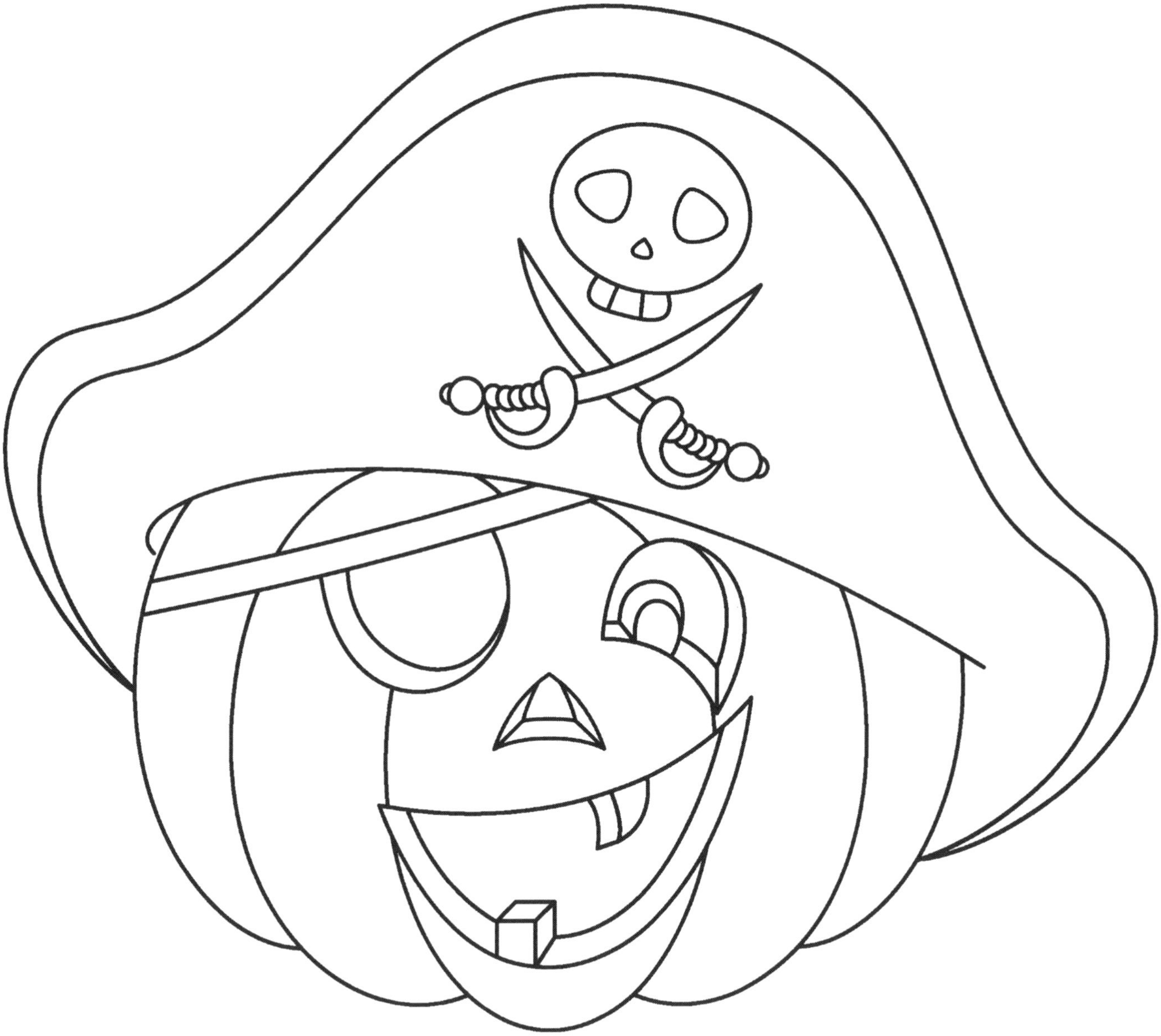

First edition: 2019
Photo credits: Shutterstock

Be sure to look for more of our fun and educational coloring and activity books for kids!

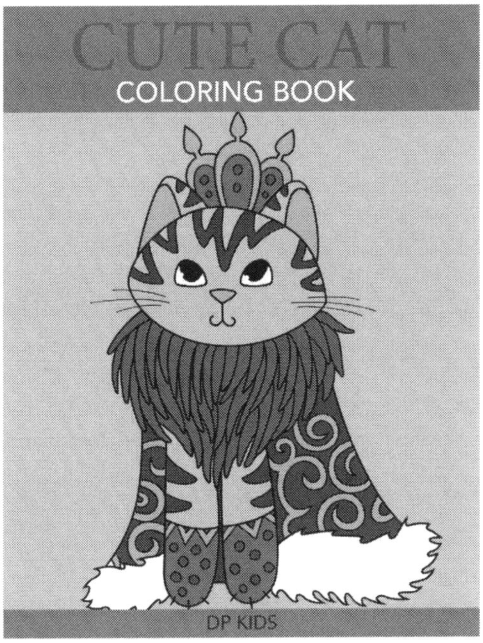

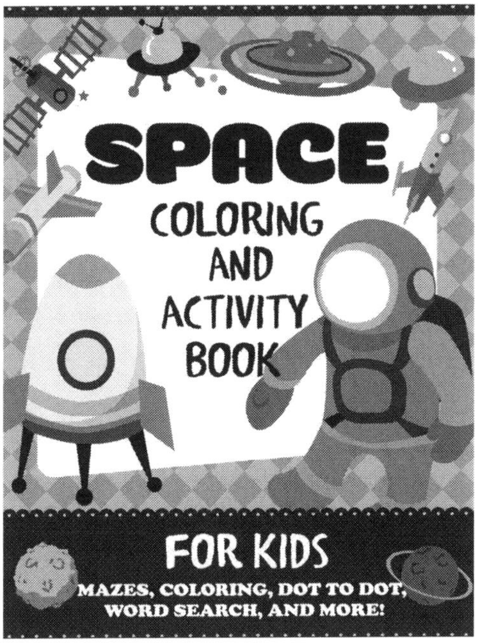

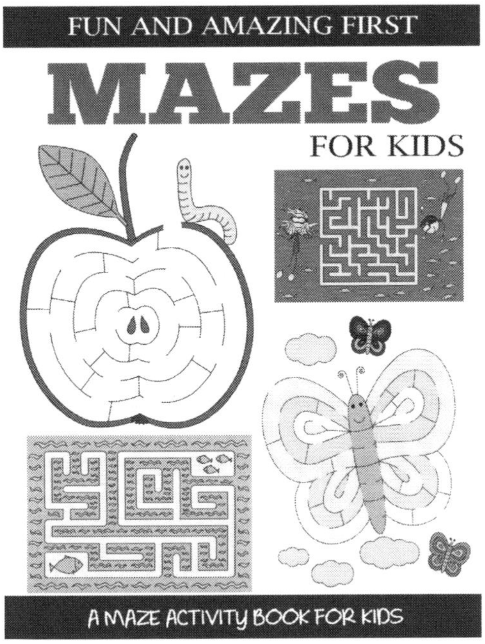

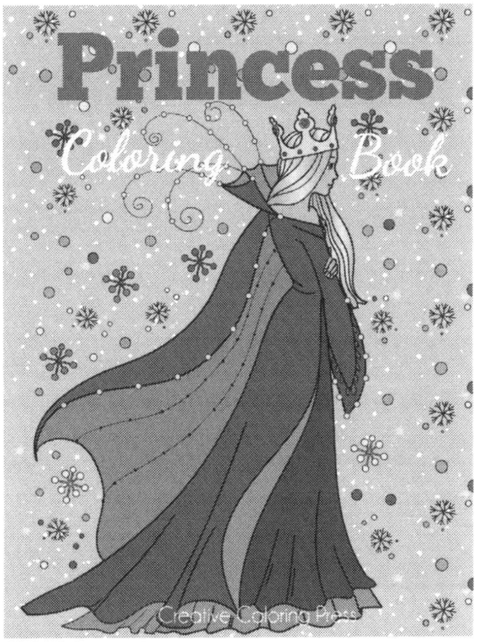